Never Trust Without Doubt

SANDEEP CHAVAN

Published by SANDEEP CHAVAN, 2024.

NEVER TRUST WITHOUT DOUBT

First edition. November 25, 2024.

ISBN: 979-8230583387

Written by SANDEEP CHAVAN.

Table of Contents

To my beloved children,**Shravani, Aradhya, and Ninad**,

May you always navigate the complexities of trust and doubt with courage, wisdom, and integrity. This book is a reflection of what I hope you carry forward—a balanced perspective that honors both your open hearts and discerning minds. You are my greatest inspiration.

"Trust without doubt is fragile, and doubt without trust is isolating. Together, they create a bridge—a pathway to clarity, connection, and resilience in an unpredictable world."

— Sandeep Chavan

Disclaimer

The content of this book, *Never Trust Without Doubt: The Interplay Between Doubt and Trust in an Unethical World*, is intended for informational and reflective purposes only. It represents the author's original thoughts, insights, and interpretations based on personal experiences and observations. While every effort has been made to provide practical tools and frameworks, the book does not constitute professional advice in areas such as psychology, law, business, or any other specialized field.

Readers are encouraged to exercise their own judgment and discretion when applying the concepts discussed in this book. The author and publisher disclaim any liability for outcomes resulting from the use or application of the ideas, tools, or strategies presented. Individual experiences with trust and doubt may vary, and readers are advised to consider their specific circumstances when making decisions.

This book is not intended to replace professional consultation or expert advice. If you require assistance in a specific area, such as mental health, legal issues, or financial decision-making, please consult a qualified professional.

The author and publisher make no guarantees about the completeness, accuracy, or reliability of the information contained in this book. By reading and engaging with the content, the reader accepts full responsibility for their interpretations and applications of the material.

Thank you for respecting the creative work and intellectual property of the author.

Preface

Trust is often seen as a cornerstone of human connection, a bond that unites individuals, organizations, and societies. Yet, in a world where ethics are increasingly ambiguous and motives are layered with complexity, trust can no longer be assumed to exist without question. This book, *Never Trust Without Doubt: The Interplay Between Doubt and Trust in an Unethical World*, was born from a deep exploration of this evolving dynamic. It challenges the traditional notion of trust as a blind leap of faith, offering instead a balanced philosophy where doubt serves not as a hindrance, but as a necessary ally.

As I embarked on this journey, I realized that trust is not an all-or-nothing state—it is a nuanced, adaptive process shaped by context, intention, and reflection. Doubt, far from being its enemy, refines trust by anchoring it in reality. This realization led to the core idea of this book: trust must be intentional, and doubt is the tool that makes it meaningful, resilient, and sustainable.

This book is for anyone navigating relationships, decisions, or environments where trust is tested—whether in personal interactions, professional partnerships, or societal structures. It is an invitation to rethink how we approach trust, to embrace doubt as a guiding force, and to build connections that honor both integrity and self-protection.

Each chapter is designed to guide you through this journey, offering practical tools, real-world examples, and reflective exercises to help you integrate this balanced philosophy into your life. From setting boundaries to using doubt as a filter, from recovering from breaches of trust to cultivating emotional resilience, this book provides a comprehensive roadmap for mastering the art of trust in an unpredictable world.

As you read, I hope you will see that trust is not static—it is dynamic, evolving, and deeply personal. It is not just a decision; it is an art, one that requires discernment, adaptability, and, above all, courage. Through the interplay of trust and doubt, we can create relationships and decisions that are not only thoughtful but transformative.

Thank you for joining me on this journey. May this book inspire you to approach trust with both heart and mind, and to embrace doubt as the silent partner that strengthens every connection.

With gratitude,

Sandeep Chavan

Introduction - The New Face of Trust in a Flawed World

In a perfect world, trust would be simple. We'd place our faith in people, institutions, and systems with confidence, knowing they would act in our best interests with integrity and reliability. But the world we live in isn't perfect—it's complex, often unpredictable, and ethically ambiguous. The landscape of trust has changed, and so must our approach to it.

The Concept of Trust in an Uncertain World

Traditionally, trust has been seen as a straightforward expression of confidence and reliance. To trust someone was to believe in their honesty, dependability, and goodwill without much question. Trust, in this sense, was almost instinctive—a willingness to assume the best intentions of others based on shared values, social norms, or reputation. For generations, this kind of trust was often enough. We trusted teachers to educate with integrity, companies to value customer welfare, and governments to serve the public interest. Society functioned on a basic assumption that people and institutions would do their part honorably, even if only because they were accountable to the community or the law.

But as our world has grown more complex and interconnected, so have the ethical dilemmas that organizations and individuals face. The globalized flow of information, resources, and power has blurred traditional boundaries and multiplied opportunities for influence—and, unfortunately, for ethical compromise. Stories of corporate scandals, political corruption, and personal betrayals have become commonplace, each instance reshaping our understanding of what it means to trust.

We're reminded of cases like Enron, where a corporation's leaders misled employees and the public, leading to financial ruin for countless individuals. Or consider data privacy scandals involving major tech companies that appeared to prioritize profit over user welfare. In the political arena, transparency issues and hidden agendas have often eroded public confidence. Even on a personal level, social media reveals daily stories of deception and betrayal, shifting how we perceive relationships with family, friends, and colleagues.

In today's world, trust has become less about blind confidence and more about intentional choice. **Placing trust in someone or something is no longer just an act of faith; it's an exercise in balancing what we know with what we don't, what we hope for with what we observe.** We carefully evaluate who deserves our trust and under what conditions. We weigh their past actions, consider their motives, and watch for signs of consistency. Trust, now, involves a degree of realism, even skepticism—a pragmatic understanding that people and systems are not infallible and that ethical standards may not always be upheld.

This nuanced approach to trust reflects the dual reality we often face: we want to trust, but we're equally aware of the risks involved. We see this in our relationships, where we may love and rely on others but recognize the need for boundaries. We see it in workplaces, where employees want to believe in their company's mission but may need assurance through transparency and accountability. And we see it in our communities, where people want to believe in their leaders but feel compelled to question policies and motivations. Trust has become a balancing act, a weighing of confidence against caution.

Our relationships, workplaces, and communities are shaped by this new reality. It's not that people have necessarily become less trustworthy, but the stakes feel higher, and transparency is often lacking. **Ethics aren't always guaranteed, and our experiences with trust have taught us that caution is necessary.** In personal relationships, we recognize that people may have private struggles or influences that impact their ability to be fully reliable. In business, companies face pressures from stakeholders, markets, and competition that may lead to ethical compromises. And in government, leaders navigate power dynamics, interests, and ideologies that may skew their actions away from public good.

Trust in this world is a complex dance—a dynamic interplay between confidence and caution, openness and skepticism. It requires us to remain open to connection while retaining a sense of self-protection. Trusting fully and blindly might be idealistic; trusting with discernment and boundaries is realistic. Today, a leap of faith is rarely enough to build trust. Instead, trust is layered, nuanced, and adaptable, involving continuous re-evaluation.

This new perspective on trust doesn't mean we have to abandon hope in others or adopt a cynical view of the world. Rather, it calls for a mature, grounded approach—one that acknowledges the imperfections in people and systems while finding ways to engage meaningfully and safely. Trust, now, is about recognizing that people are often trying their best within flawed systems, that organizations may have to navigate complex priorities, and that integrity is sometimes a moving target.

Navigating trust in this world requires us to embrace both trust and doubt as two sides of the same coin. **Doubt is not a sign of weakness in trust but a vital component of it**—a way to keep our expectations reasonable and our vulnerabilities in check. By integrating doubt into our trust, we allow room for discernment, for gradual growth in confidence, and for setting boundaries that protect us. This isn't the traditional notion of trust as a leap of faith; it's a new model of trust as a resilient, adaptive process that meets the challenges of a morally complex world.

As we move forward, this book will explore how to cultivate this evolved form of trust. We'll look at practical strategies for balancing trust with discernment, for verifying intentions without slipping into cynicism, and for building relationships that can thrive even in ethically uncertain landscapes. This new face of trust is one that allows us to connect meaningfully while staying grounded, to trust others while honoring our own need for clarity and caution.

Doubt: Not an Obstacle but a Partner in Trust

In this complex landscape, **doubt emerges not as an obstacle to trust but as its essential partner**. Traditionally, doubt has been cast as the antagonist in the story of trust, the opposing force that undermines faith and erodes confidence. We're often told that doubt is a sign of weakness or insecurity, something to overcome in our quest for deeper connections and reliance on others. But in today's world, where ethical certainties are rare, doubt is actually a powerful ally—a quiet strength that keeps trust grounded, realistic, and resilient.

Doubt allows us to approach trust with our eyes open, to engage fully without losing sight of the need for caution. It's a subtle reminder that people, circumstances, and systems are rarely flawless. In fact, it's **doubt that makes trust possible in environments where ethical behavior isn't a given**. Without doubt, trust could become blind, leaving us vulnerable to disappointment, manipulation, or harm. Doubt, therefore, doesn't weaken trust; it refines and fortifies it. It keeps trust balanced and intentional, helping us navigate relationships and situations thoughtfully.

Imagine standing on the edge of a river with only a narrow bridge to cross. If the bridge were solid and sturdy, you'd walk across without hesitation, confident in its ability to support you. Trust would come easily. But what if the bridge looks less stable? The wood might be worn, the railing shaky, and beneath you, the river rushes with intensity. In this moment, doubt doesn't prevent you from crossing; instead, it guides **how you cross**. You test the planks with your foot, keep a hand on the railing, and step cautiously, aware of each move you make. You may even pause halfway, assessing whether it's safe to proceed. This is how doubt functions within trust: it allows us to place confidence with a measured approach, ensuring that our trust is deliberate and grounded in reality.

Doubt as a Check and Balance for Trust

Doubt acts as a natural check and balance within the process of trust. By questioning, observing, and verifying, doubt encourages us to keep our expectations realistic. When doubt coexists with trust, it prompts us to set boundaries and monitor outcomes, allowing trust to develop in a secure, supported way. This type of trust is dynamic—it doesn't expect perfection but adapts to the changing realities and evolving behaviors of those we trust.

In relationships, for example, doubt doesn't necessarily mean that we distrust someone. Instead, it reminds us to remain aware, to notice shifts in behavior, and to communicate openly about concerns as they arise. When trusting someone with sensitive information or shared responsibilities, doubt may lead us to clarify expectations or check in periodically, reinforcing the foundation of trust. This ongoing process, shaped by both confidence and caution, builds a trust that isn't easily shaken by the inevitable complexities of human relationships.

In business, doubt encourages us to establish verification systems, to ask questions, and to seek transparency. It reminds us to monitor progress, require documentation, and ensure accountability. Here, doubt protects trust by preventing it from becoming blind reliance. By allowing us to trust with intention, doubt ensures that trust isn't an idealistic assumption but a sustainable, balanced engagement based on observed integrity and clear communication.

Trust with Doubt: A Trust with Depth

Trust that includes doubt is trust with depth. It acknowledges that people and situations are complex, that ethical behavior can't always be taken for granted, and that circumstances are subject to change. Instead of diminishing trust, doubt refines it. Doubt acts as an internal compass, helping us gauge when to proceed, when to hold back, and when to reassess. It gives us a framework to trust wisely, preventing us from placing blind faith in situations where caution might be warranted.

Trust with doubt is like navigating with a well-calibrated compass: it doesn't allow us to be swept up in every emotion or to assume certainty where there is none. Instead, it provides direction, helping us discern which paths are safe, which require caution, and which may not be worth pursuing at all. This trust is adaptable, able to withstand disappointments or changes in circumstances. If someone we trusted falters, doubt allows us to reevaluate, to adjust our expectations, and to reset boundaries, maintaining the integrity of trust without losing hope in others altogether.

In environments where ethics are unclear or where the stakes are high, doubt becomes a protector of trust. It guards us against overcommitting or being misled. **By allowing doubt to coexist with trust, we create a form of trust that is sustainable, adaptable, and, above all, resilient.** This trust is realistic and grounded, recognizing both the potential and limitations of those we trust. When doubt plays a role, trust becomes a steady presence that can withstand the pressures of an imperfect world.

The Role of Doubt in Building Resilient Trust

Allowing doubt to partner with trust enables us to engage with others without compromising our own boundaries or values. It teaches us to trust with integrity, knowing when to extend confidence and when to retain caution. This kind of trust doesn't seek guarantees but thrives in the balance between faith and discernment. We can approach relationships, work, and communities with an open heart and a critical mind, knowing that doubt is there to protect us.

In a world where ethical guarantees are few, trusting with doubt doesn't make us cynical; it makes us wise. It acknowledges reality while leaving room for genuine connection. This isn't the type of trust that demands flawless loyalty or unbroken promises. Instead, it allows for imperfection, understanding that people can have good intentions but may falter. Doubt reminds us to be vigilant, to watch and learn, but it also allows us to trust with hope and openness, ready to adjust as needed.

In the following chapters, we'll explore how this interplay of trust and doubt can be applied practically. We'll look at techniques for setting boundaries, ways to verify actions without undermining relationships, and strategies for engaging in trust that is both open and self-protective. Together, trust and doubt create a balanced approach that prepares us for life's uncertainties, allowing us to engage meaningfully without sacrificing our security.

In this sense, **doubt is a wise companion to trust**. It guides us, reminds us to stay grounded, and strengthens our confidence by ensuring that our trust is earned, not assumed. As we embrace this partnership, we unlock a new way of relating to others—one that is dynamic, resilient, and capable of thriving even in the most challenging environments.

The Interplay of Trust and Doubt in Challenging Environments

This partnership between trust and doubt is what enables us to navigate complex environments thoughtfully. In settings where ethics are unclear or where integrity can't be taken for granted, doubt becomes an essential guide. Rather than obstructing trust, doubt helps us make **informed choices about**

where to place our trust and how much of it to offer. This interplay allows us to engage with others while maintaining our boundaries, to collaborate without becoming complacent, and to build connections without compromising our values.

Consider the nuanced, dynamic nature of trust in a workplace where transparency is inconsistent, or in a friendship where someone's reliability has been questionable. In these cases, doubt doesn't necessarily mean withdrawing trust entirely. Instead, it suggests an approach rooted in intention and discernment. For instance, you may trust a colleague to handle specific tasks within their expertise but refrain from sharing sensitive information until you observe more consistent, reliable behavior. This conditional trust allows you to engage productively without leaving yourself exposed.

Similarly, in personal relationships, doubt doesn't have to signal distrust; it can simply mean allowing trust to grow gradually, in stages that reflect the other person's actions and commitments. You may choose to keep a friend at arm's length initially, engaging casually and allowing the relationship to evolve as mutual trust is established. By approaching with caution, you give the relationship room to grow based on trust that is **earned rather than assumed**.

In this way, **doubt shines as a tool of discernment**, guiding us to extend trust thoughtfully and in a way that respects our values. It encourages us to watch for signs, to verify actions, and to observe patterns over time. Instead of placing blind faith in a situation or relationship, doubt allows us to base trust on **evidence, consistency, and a deeper understanding** of those involved. This approach strengthens trust by grounding it in reality rather than mere hope.

In environments where ethics may waver, doubt acts as an anchor, ensuring that we can trust without feeling overly vulnerable to betrayal or disappointment. It gives us the space to engage meaningfully while staying aware, balancing our openness with a sense of caution that keeps our trust protected. This balance becomes especially crucial in high-stakes situations, where a single breach of trust can have significant consequences. By allowing doubt to inform our trust, we maintain a stable footing even when external circumstances are unpredictable or challenging.

Real-World Examples of Trust-Doubt Interplay

In the workplace, for example, an employee might need to trust their manager to guide their career path. However, if that manager's behavior has been inconsistent or self-serving, the employee's trust must be tempered by caution. Rather than fully relying on the manager for career growth, the employee might choose to seek mentorship elsewhere or document their contributions carefully. Here, doubt doesn't obstruct the professional relationship but adds a layer of resilience, allowing the employee to trust in specific areas while staying mindful of potential conflicts.

Or consider a family business where trust is typically implicit but occasionally strained by competing interests. Family members may trust each other to act in the business's best interest but might still put safeguards in place, like regular audits or decision-making protocols, to ensure transparency. This doesn't mean family members distrust one another; it simply reflects an understanding that even in close relationships, trust benefits from accountability and structure. By incorporating doubt as a check and balance, trust becomes a stable, reliable foundation rather than a fragile assumption.

In friendships or romantic relationships, this interplay allows us to remain open-hearted without giving up our sense of self-protection. We might deeply care for someone and enjoy their company but still choose to watch for signs of consistency, honesty, and respect. Doubt doesn't mean we assume the worst of others—it means we're conscious of the complexities of human nature and the pressures that people face, and we're prepared to recalibrate trust if needed. This balance allows relationships to flourish without leaving us unguarded against disappointment or hurt.

Building Trust Wisely: The Role of Evidence and Understanding

Doubt allows us to build trust based on evidence rather than assumptions. It invites us to look for actions that align with words, for promises that turn into follow-through. This approach helps us avoid the pitfalls of idealizing others or expecting perfection, enabling us to place trust that feels steady and reasonable. Over time, as we gather evidence and understanding, trust deepens naturally, supported by a solid foundation of observed integrity.

When trust is based on consistent actions rather than blind faith, it becomes resilient to external shifts and minor setbacks. We can face disagreements, misunderstandings, or even mistakes without losing trust completely because we know it was built thoughtfully. In challenging environments, where people's motivations may vary or circumstances can change, this trust-with-doubt model offers stability. It keeps us connected without making us overly reliant, engaged but still discerning.

The Interplay of Trust and Doubt as a Framework for Boundaries

One of the most practical outcomes of balancing trust and doubt is the ability to set **clear, adaptable boundaries**. When we know that doubt has a role in our trusting relationships, we're more likely to establish guidelines for what we expect and what we'll accept. This is especially useful in environments where ethics may be compromised or where misunderstandings are common. By defining boundaries based on our comfort level, we can participate fully without feeling vulnerable to ethical lapses or interpersonal conflicts.

Boundaries allow us to engage in relationships while retaining autonomy and self-respect. For instance, in a collaborative project, doubt might encourage us to set specific terms for accountability, ensuring that each team member's contributions are documented and recognized. In personal relationships, boundaries shaped by trust and doubt could mean agreeing to open, honest communication while reserving the right to reassess if that communication falters. Boundaries become a way to honor both our willingness to trust and our need for self-protection, creating a framework that's supportive rather than restrictive.

Trust Without Vulnerability to Betrayal

In environments where ethics are uncertain, the interplay of trust and doubt allows us to trust without feeling overly vulnerable. It helps us remain aware, evaluating the trustworthiness of those around us without resorting to suspicion or cynicism. This balance means we're not afraid to engage fully, but we're also prepared to step back if circumstances or behaviors change. Trust becomes an active choice rather than a passive assumption, empowering us to adjust and adapt as needed.

When trust is informed by doubt, it doesn't break down easily at the first sign of difficulty. Doubt gives us the flexibility to respond thoughtfully to challenges, recalibrating rather than retreating. We may trust people to varying degrees, or in specific areas, but doubt reminds us to keep assessing as situations evolve. This form of trust feels grounded and safe because it's not dependent on unwavering belief; it's adaptable, resilient, and capable of surviving change.

Moving Forward: Exploring the Practical Interplay of Trust and Doubt

In the chapters that follow, we'll explore the interplay of trust and doubt in greater depth. We'll examine how doubt can act as a safety net, allowing us to test trust gradually without risking disappointment or harm. We'll look at how **conditional trust** empowers us to set boundaries, making trust a measured choice rather than an assumption. We'll also explore **principle-based trust**, a form of trust grounded in shared values and standards that remains stable even when people may fall short.

Through practical tools, reflective exercises, and real-world examples, you'll learn how to cultivate a trust that feels safe, adaptable, and ethically grounded—even in challenging environments. This approach will enable you to build trust in a way that aligns with your values, empowers your choices, and enhances your connections.

In a world filled with complexity and unpredictability, the partnership between trust and doubt offers a balanced approach to relationships, work, and personal growth. By embracing doubt as a part of trust, we gain the freedom to connect meaningfully without compromising our sense of security. This is the path to resilient, thoughtful trust—the kind of trust that can thrive even in the most challenging environments.

Conclusion

Trust is no longer a simple act of faith; it has evolved into an artful balance that requires both heart and mind. In a world where ethics can be ambiguous and motivations unclear, **trust without doubt can be naïve, leaving us vulnerable**

to harm or disappointment, but doubt without trust can be isolating, cutting us off from meaningful connections and shared experiences. The key lies in **combining the two**—trust and doubt—in a way that enables us to engage with the world thoughtfully and responsibly.

When we bring doubt into our practice of trust, we enrich it. Doubt is not the enemy of trust; it is its **protector and companion**. It encourages us to approach trust with an open mind but also with a grounded awareness, allowing us to extend confidence to others without overlooking the importance of caution. In this way, trust becomes not a leap of faith into the unknown but a steady bridge that we build, plank by plank, based on evidence, observation, and mutual respect. This deliberate approach makes trust resilient, adaptable, and prepared to withstand the inevitable ups and downs of real life.

Where there is doubt, there is the possibility of trust—not a trust that is blind and fragile, but one that is cautious, resilient, and profoundly empowering. This form of trust doesn't ask us to ignore our instincts or sacrifice our boundaries. Instead, it invites us to engage mindfully, placing trust where it is earned and adjusting it as needed. It allows us to trust with a sense of autonomy and security, knowing that our trust is based on a balanced view of both the potential and limitations of others.

In relationships, workplaces, and communities, trust grounded in doubt provides a foundation that is both stable and flexible. In personal relationships, it means approaching with care, setting boundaries, and allowing trust to grow gradually as consistency is demonstrated. In professional settings, it means seeking transparency, verifying commitments, and engaging in open communication to align intentions and actions. In each of these contexts, doubt ensures that trust remains reasonable, empowering us to stay present and engaged without sacrificing our sense of self-protection.

This is the new face of trust in a flawed world—a trust that respects the complexities of human behavior, the pressures of modern life, and the reality of ethical uncertainty. It's a trust that doesn't demand perfection but is prepared to adapt and adjust as circumstances evolve. In this form, trust becomes an adaptable tool, a resource we can draw upon to navigate challenges and build meaningful relationships even in unpredictable or ethically ambiguous environments.

Practicing trust in this balanced way requires self-awareness, patience, and a commitment to growth. It asks us to look at trust not as a one-time decision but as an evolving process, one that changes as we learn, observe, and reassess. It requires us to remain open to others while also staying true to our values, knowing that the world we live in is neither perfect nor entirely predictable. This balanced trust lets us connect deeply, collaborate effectively, and create spaces of mutual respect, even when circumstances are less than ideal.

By allowing doubt to inform our trust, we cultivate a trust that is **resilient, ethical, and wise**. This approach to trust is not about isolating ourselves with skepticism, nor is it about surrendering our caution in favor of blind optimism. Instead, it's about finding the middle ground where trust becomes a dynamic practice, one that can adapt to the realities of the world while honoring our need for security, clarity, and respect.

To cultivate trust in this way is to embrace both vulnerability and strength. We acknowledge that trusting involves some risk, but we mitigate that risk by allowing doubt to guide us. We open ourselves to others, but we do so mindfully, recognizing that trust is not just about the other person's reliability but also about our own ability to discern, to assess, and to adjust.

In a world where ethical behavior isn't always guaranteed, this balanced form of trust is a tool that empowers us. It frees us to engage without fear, to connect without losing ourselves, and to invest in relationships and endeavors that reflect our values. By embracing this duality of trust and doubt, we allow ourselves to experience the full richness of human connection without compromising our need for security and clarity.

This is a trust worth cultivating—a trust that honors both our hope and our discernment, our openness and our caution. It is a trust that meets the complexities of our world with resilience and wisdom, a trust that can thrive even in the face of challenges, disappointments, or ethical uncertainty. This new face of trust, grounded in the balanced interplay of heart and mind, is a powerful and transformative force, one that can guide us toward relationships and environments that are both meaningful and safe.

As you move forward, consider how you might practice this balance of trust and doubt in your own life. Reflect on the relationships, commitments, and environments where trust has felt challenging and explore ways to bring doubt into the process as a tool for clarity and protection. Use the strategies in this book as a framework, adapting them to your unique experiences and needs. Allow yourself to trust where trust is earned, to hold back when necessary, and to build connections that are both enriching and secure.

In a flawed world, we cannot always control the actions or intentions of others, but we can choose how we engage with them. By cultivating trust with the guidance of doubt, we choose to engage with awareness, to open up thoughtfully, and to build a life grounded in both integrity and insight. This trust, strengthened by discernment and resilience, is the kind that sustains us, empowers us, and allows us to move confidently through the complexities of a world that is, indeed, imperfect but still full of possibility.

1: Trust Reimagined—Why Doubt Is Essential

Trust is often portrayed as a leap of faith—a simple, unquestioning belief in someone's intentions or capabilities. But in today's world, where motives are often layered, and ethics are not always guaranteed, this traditional notion of trust feels incomplete. To navigate the complexities of modern relationships, trust must be reimagined. Doubt, far from being its enemy, becomes an essential ally—a force that refines and strengthens trust by keeping it grounded in reality. In this chapter, we will explore why trust is no longer about blind confidence but about thoughtful engagement, where doubt serves as a tool for clarity, discernment, and resilience.

Redefining Trust: A Flexible, Intentional Process

In the traditional sense, trust is often perceived as an unquestioning leap of faith, a complete surrender to confidence in another person or system. This type of trust assumes a level of certainty—a belief that people are inherently reliable, that promises will be kept, and that ethical behavior is a given. In this model, trust is nearly automatic, a default setting we apply to those around us based on initial impressions, social roles, or past relationships. We trust our friends, family, colleagues, and leaders simply because we feel we should. But in today's world, such a perspective can feel naive and even risky. As we navigate an increasingly complex society, where motives are often layered and ethics not always guaranteed, trust requires redefinition. **No longer is trust a passive assumption; instead, it has become a flexible, intentional process that we navigate with awareness and discernment.**

Redefining trust means shifting from the idea of trust as an absolute, unwavering state to viewing it as a thoughtful, active choice. Trust in this reimagined form is not a singular, all-or-nothing decision; rather, it is a **dynamic balance between openness and restraint, between extending confidence and exercising caution**. This flexible model of trust encourages us to adapt our levels of trust based on changing circumstances, to reassess our commitments over time, and to approach trust as a gradual, evolving relationship rather than a one-time leap of faith.

In this new perspective, trust is something we build **intentionally and incrementally**. It doesn't call for blind faith but instead invites us to be both thoughtful and selective about where, how, and to whom we extend our trust. Just as we wouldn't dive into deep water without knowing how to swim, redefined trust encourages us to step forward cautiously, assessing depth and conditions as we go. We trust not out of habit but out of choice, weighing each situation to determine how much trust is warranted and how much caution is wise.

The Bridge of Trust: Built Gradually, Tested Over Time

Think of trust as a bridge. In the past, we might have built that bridge in a day, expecting it to hold firm without further inspection. Once trust was established, it was assumed to be strong and stable, needing little upkeep or examination. But in our current landscape, the bridge of trust is not something we rush to build overnight. Instead, it's constructed **plank by plank**, reinforced over time through mutual actions, observed consistency, and occasional reassessments. We test it as we go, adding support where needed and adjusting as we see signs of wear or change.

This analogy highlights the intentional nature of modern trust. Just as a bridge requires maintenance and inspection to ensure it remains safe, so too does trust need periodic evaluation. **Trust is no longer a static structure**; it's a living framework, one that needs to be nurtured, adjusted, and sometimes fortified based on experience and observation. We don't simply declare trust and expect it to last indefinitely; we allow it to grow, develop, and adapt as circumstances and relationships evolve. If we notice gaps or weaknesses, we address them. If our trust bridge becomes shaky, we reinforce it with open communication, boundary-setting, or perhaps a reassessment of expectations.

This kind of trust is **intentional and ongoing**, constructed with both optimism and prudence. It recognizes that people are complex, that situations can shift, and that challenges will arise. It accepts that ethical challenges are part of life and that trust must be resilient enough to withstand the natural fluctuations of human behavior and circumstance. In this way, trust becomes less of a risk and more of an adaptable, sustainable foundation.

Empowerment Through Intentional Trust

This intentional approach to trust is profoundly empowering. **Instead of leaving us vulnerable, it gives us agency**, allowing us to decide how much trust we offer, in what ways, and to whom. We're no longer placing our full faith in others without a second thought; instead, we're actively choosing to trust in ways that feel safe, measured, and appropriate to each unique relationship or setting.

In personal relationships, this means we may trust a friend with casual conversations or fun outings, but withhold deeper trust until we observe their ability to keep confidences, show empathy, and demonstrate reliability. We are no longer obligated to give complete trust based on familiarity or social expectation; rather, we allow trust to build as each person earns it. Similarly, in a professional setting, we may trust a coworker with specific tasks based on their skills or expertise but choose to verify their work before relying on it for critical projects. Over time, as we observe their consistency, our trust might grow, and we may extend more responsibilities. **By reimagining trust as a flexible process, we create a trust that serves us well**, a trust that is capable of adapting and growing as circumstances demand.

This new approach also allows us to protect ourselves from the disappointments and setbacks that can come with blind trust. When we build trust incrementally, we have time to adjust if something doesn't feel right or if the other person doesn't meet our expectations. We can recalibrate without the heartbreak of a major betrayal, as our cautious approach has allowed us to preserve some distance and discernment. Trust becomes a resource we manage rather than a vulnerability we expose, empowering us to navigate relationships with confidence, integrity, and self-respect.

Trust as a Balance of Openness and Restraint

With this redefined model, trust becomes a **balance of openness and restraint**. We can extend confidence without completely letting down our guard, and we can open ourselves to others without abandoning our boundaries. This balance allows us to remain engaged with the world, receptive to meaningful connections and collaborative experiences, while still honoring our own need for protection and clarity. Trust doesn't require us to give up our discernment; in fact, it flourishes because of it.

In a world where motives aren't always clear and where ethical behavior may vary from one person to the next, this balanced approach lets us approach trust practically. We no longer have to choose between blind faith and total skepticism; instead, we navigate the middle ground where trust becomes a **measured, conscious choice**. By allowing ourselves to trust gradually, with boundaries and checkpoints along the way, we maintain control over our emotional investments. We are open enough to experience the benefits of trust but aware enough to protect ourselves from unnecessary harm.

This approach is also incredibly practical in professional environments, where collaboration and interdependence are essential but where full transparency and accountability are not always present. By extending trust selectively and conditionally, we can build effective working relationships without overexposing ourselves to risks. For instance, we might work closely with a colleague on a project while maintaining a professional boundary in areas outside the project scope. This allows us to engage meaningfully without losing sight of our own boundaries or compromising our values.

The Flexibility of Reimagined Trust

The beauty of this flexible, intentional trust is its **adaptability**. Because it's built on observation and reassessment, it can withstand the natural changes that occur in relationships and environments. As we get to know someone better or as circumstances shift, we can adjust our trust to match the new reality. If someone shows increased reliability, we can deepen our trust, knowing it's earned. If someone falters, we can pull back without feeling destabilized, recognizing that trust is a spectrum, not an absolute.

This flexible approach is particularly valuable in a world where rapid changes are the norm. In business, technology, and even social environments, situations can evolve quickly, and the ability to adjust trust in real-time is a strength. We are not forced into rigid patterns of trust or mistrust; instead, we allow our trust to ebb and flow in response to actual experience, remaining flexible without becoming cynical.

The Power of Reimagined Trust in Our Lives

Ultimately, this redefined approach to trust **empowers us to navigate our world with intention and discernment**. We are no longer passive recipients of other people's promises or intentions; we are active participants in shaping the quality and depth of our relationships. By practicing trust as an evolving process, we gain control over the choices we make and the connections we form. We engage with people and systems thoughtfully, choosing to trust where it feels right and withholding trust where it feels necessary.

In a world where ethics are not always clear and certainty is rarely assured, this model of trust serves us well. It lets us experience connection, collaboration, and closeness without losing our sense of independence and protection. We cultivate a trust that is both **generous and guarded**, a trust that reflects our values, respects our boundaries, and adapts to the unique nature of each relationship.

Trust, redefined in this way, is not a compromise but a choice. It allows us to remain open to the world's possibilities while honoring the reality of its complexities. In the chapters that follow, we will delve into practical ways to apply this flexible, intentional model of trust, exploring how to establish boundaries, incorporate doubt, and build a resilient foundation for trust that feels both safe and enriching.

By approaching trust as an art rather than an assumption, we transform it from a potential vulnerability into a source of strength and stability. This reimagined trust becomes a powerful tool for navigating life's challenges, capable of supporting us as we connect, collaborate, and grow in a world that is, at once, both beautiful and flawed.

Doubt as the Strength Behind Trust

In this reimagined view of trust, **doubt becomes not a threat but an ally**, one that keeps our trust rooted in reality rather than wishful thinking. Traditionally, doubt has been viewed as something to overcome—a barrier that holds us back from giving ourselves fully to others or from placing confidence in relationships and commitments. But in today's complex world, **doubt acts as a balancing force**, allowing us to trust carefully and selectively. Far from weakening trust, it actually strengthens it, transforming it from a blind leap of faith into a nuanced, thoughtful decision that we make with awareness and clarity.

Doubt is a tool of discernment, particularly valuable in settings where motivations may be unclear, where intentions can be complex, or where moral certainties are absent. Rather than seeing doubt as an enemy to trust, we can embrace it as a companion, one that guides us to look beyond surface-level promises and words, examining instead the actions, behaviors, and consistency of those we're considering trusting. Doubt enables us to approach trust from a position of strength, empowering us to engage meaningfully while staying grounded in reality.

Doubt empowers trust by acting as a natural safeguard. When we incorporate doubt, we sidestep the pitfalls of blind faith, protecting ourselves from placing trust where it may not be warranted. Instead of feeling obligated to trust automatically, we're encouraged to pause, assess, and ensure that trust aligns with our values and boundaries. Doubt helps us maintain a sense of control over our trust, giving us the time and space to verify if the relationship, commitment, or engagement truly deserves our confidence.

Consider a workplace setting, for instance. You may be asked to trust a colleague with an important project or sensitive information, but doubt may prompt you to examine their past actions, check for signs of reliability, and perhaps start with smaller tasks before entrusting them fully. **Doubt, in this case, doesn't prevent trust but enhances it**. It ensures that your trust is placed with intention and that you are protected against potential oversights or misunderstandings. If the colleague's past behavior has shown consistency and integrity, doubt allows you to proceed with greater confidence. But if you observe inconsistencies or signs of unreliability, doubt serves as a signal to hold back, adjust expectations, or set boundaries.

In personal relationships, doubt similarly plays a protective role. When someone's words don't align with their actions, doubt encourages us to pause and reassess rather than rushing to trust based on our hopes or assumptions. This thoughtful application of doubt enables us to recognize red flags early on, helping us avoid investing too much trust in relationships that may not be secure or supportive. Rather than blindly giving ourselves to others, we're able to engage with discernment, allowing trust to grow gradually and organically as the relationship proves itself worthy over time.

Grounded and Cautious Trust Through Doubt

This thoughtful approach enables trust to be **grounded and cautious**, a trust that is built on real-world evidence rather than mere aspiration. Instead of jumping to trust based solely on hopes or assumptions, we engage with it as a gradual, evolving choice. **Doubt doesn't mean we lack trust; it means we're intentional about how we trust**. By incorporating doubt, we allow ourselves to trust in ways that are sustainable and aligned with the dynamics of real-life situations. This form of trust is adaptable, capable of shifting in response to changing circumstances or new information, making it far more likely to endure.

Rather than setting ourselves up for potential betrayal or disappointment, doubt encourages us to take measured steps, testing trust as we go. With each step, we assess whether the person or situation aligns with our values and expectations, and if not, we're free to adjust. In this way, doubt doesn't undermine trust but reinforces it, creating a foundation that is flexible yet strong, responsive yet secure.

Imagine, for example, the process of trusting a new business partner. Traditional trust might urge us to take their promises at face value, assuming they will act in good faith because they've given us their word. But **with doubt as a companion**, we take a more measured approach. We might look into their past partnerships, examine how they have treated others in similar situations, and possibly start with a smaller collaboration to build trust gradually. This isn't mistrust; it's prudent, grounded trust, based on verification and thoughtful observation rather than blind assumption. In this way, doubt serves as a guide, allowing us to extend trust carefully while still honoring our need for security and caution.

Doubt as an Essential Part of Trust in Uncertain Settings

In uncertain settings—be it in business, friendships, or even interactions with public institutions—**doubt becomes a crucial part of trust, ensuring that we**

are not simply relying on others' promises but actively assessing whether those promises align with their actions. Doubt helps us set boundaries, define expectations, and monitor consistency, allowing trust to grow on a foundation of accountability. This process helps us engage fully while protecting ourselves from the risks that come from unexamined trust.

For instance, in a public institution where transparency is limited, doubt allows us to advocate for more information, ask questions, and stay involved as engaged citizens. We can support the institution's initiatives, but we remain alert to discrepancies, keeping ourselves informed and ready to call for accountability if needed. Doubt, in this case, doesn't mean we lack trust in the institution but that we are committed to ensuring that our trust is based on verified integrity rather than assumptions.

In personal relationships, doubt can similarly provide a safety net. When we meet new friends or romantic partners, doubt allows us to pace ourselves, observing how they treat others, how they communicate, and how they handle challenges. This gives us a clearer picture of their character and reliability, helping us build trust based on observation and understanding rather than simply emotional connection. By giving trust a chance to grow gradually, doubt protects us from becoming overly attached too soon and allows the relationship to develop naturally.

Creating Resilient Trust Through Doubt

By introducing doubt as an essential part of the process, **we create a version of trust that is resilient, grounded, and far more likely to withstand the tests of time and complexity**. Trust that incorporates doubt is built with flexibility, able to adjust as situations change, and it holds up to scrutiny because it's based on evidence rather than assumption. This form of trust is more sustainable because it respects the unpredictability of people and environments. It allows us to remain open and engaged without feeling vulnerable to shifts in circumstances or surprises in behavior.

Doubt also reinforces trust by encouraging transparency and communication. When doubt is part of trust, we are more likely to discuss expectations openly, ask for clarity, and create accountability. This transparent approach builds mutual respect and understanding, as both parties are aware of the standards being upheld. Doubt doesn't mean we're suspicious; it means we care about the integrity of our relationships, ensuring that trust is actively maintained.

The Balance of Trust and Doubt: A New Strength

In this redefined model, doubt doesn't erode trust; it fortifies it. By allowing doubt to coexist with trust, we cultivate a trust that is less fragile, less likely to be shaken by challenges or betrayals. Doubt gives trust a backbone, a structure that prevents it from collapsing under the weight of idealism or unmet expectations. This balanced trust is a strong trust, one that allows us to navigate uncertain environments with confidence and poise.

Doubt gives us the freedom to trust without feeling naïve, to connect without compromising our sense of self, and to engage with others while honoring our own boundaries. It allows us to cultivate relationships that are both deep and secure, professional engagements that are both collaborative and clear, and connections that are both meaningful and respectful.

As we continue exploring this model of trust, consider how doubt might serve as an ally in your own life. Let it be a tool that empowers you to trust wisely, enabling you to engage meaningfully while remaining protected. By balancing trust with doubt, we create a form of trust that is grounded, resilient, and prepared for the complex, ever-changing world in which we live.

Realistic and Sustainable Trust through Doubt

By incorporating doubt, **we create a form of trust that is both realistic and sustainable**. This doesn't mean we're pessimistic or predisposed to distrust; rather, it means that our trust is built with an understanding of human nature—recognizing that circumstances change, pressures arise, and people can falter. Trust, when reinforced by doubt, becomes adaptable to these shifting realities. It becomes more than a single, rigid commitment; it transforms into an evolving relationship that is resilient enough to withstand the natural ups and downs of life.

Trust built with doubt is not easily shattered by a single failure or mistake. Instead of seeing trust as an all-or-nothing proposition, we view it as a flexible framework that can recalibrate when needed, adjusting expectations while maintaining the core relationship. If someone we trust falls short in one instance, we are not left devastated or cynical; rather, we have the flexibility to take a step back, assess the situation, and decide how best to proceed. This trust is designed to bend, not break, allowing us to forgive, to communicate openly about issues, and to re-establish boundaries as needed.

Mutual Accountability and Trust Built on Reciprocity

Trust grounded in doubt also encourages a dynamic of **mutual accountability**. When we trust conditionally, we set clear expectations with those we trust, defining what actions, behaviors, and communication we need to see in order for that trust to grow. By incorporating doubt, we make trust an active, two-way commitment rather than a passive assumption. We communicate openly about what we expect and need, encouraging others to meet those expectations in a spirit of mutual respect. This prompts others to recognize that trust is something earned and maintained, not something automatically assumed or taken for granted.

This **reciprocity fosters stronger, more resilient relationships**. It sets the stage for a trust that is grounded in actions rather than mere words, allowing both parties to feel secure and respected. In this environment, when trust is reciprocated, it builds a foundation of mutual respect and understanding that enhances both the quality and stability of the relationship. It also invites transparency and authenticity, as both sides are clear about their expectations and have agreed to be accountable to them.

Consider the dynamics of a **family business**, for example, where trust between family members is critical but must also be accompanied by accountability. With doubt as part of the equation, family members might agree to periodic reviews of financial records, transparent decision-making processes, or shared responsibilities. This doesn't imply a lack of trust in each other; rather, it shows a commitment to sustaining trust through transparent practices and ethical boundaries. By allowing doubt to guide these structures, trust is reinforced, not weakened. Family members know they can rely on each other, but this reliance is grounded in a framework that encourages responsible choices and mitigates risks associated with potential conflicts of interest. In this sense, doubt does not diminish familial trust but preserves it by setting up guardrails for healthy, sustainable interaction.

Doubt as a Tool for Flexibility in Romantic Relationships

In romantic relationships, doubt plays a similar and equally vital role. Rather than assuming lifelong trust based solely on initial feelings, couples can allow doubt to guide their growth, keeping trust both realistic and adaptable. **This realistic approach to trust doesn't assume perfection** but is open to working through imperfections as they arise. Couples may establish regular check-ins, discuss concerns or boundaries openly, and respect each other's independence. By doing so, trust becomes a flexible and dynamic process—one that grows alongside the individuals within the relationship.

Doubt in a romantic context allows each partner to feel free to express concerns and adjust expectations as needed. If a partner struggles with a particular issue, doubt enables the other to communicate openly, offering support without setting unrealistic expectations. This ongoing dialogue makes trust adaptable, allowing both individuals to adjust and grow without feeling pressured to meet unyielding standards. **This adaptability enables the relationship to survive misunderstandings, changes, and challenges**, because trust was built on a foundation that is resilient rather than brittle.

In this sense, doubt empowers both partners to bring their full, authentic selves into the relationship, knowing that trust is not contingent upon perfection but upon communication, integrity, and commitment. This approach ultimately leads to a **deeper, more sustainable connection**, as each partner feels valued and supported, even during times of change or difficulty.

Doubt as an Invitation to Growth and Self-Reflection

By embracing doubt as part of trust, **we open ourselves up to growth**—both within our relationships and within ourselves. This kind of trust isn't static; it is ever-changing, reflecting the natural ebbs and flows of relationships, environments, and personal development. Doubt invites us to re-evaluate our trust periodically, to ask whether it still serves us, whether boundaries need to shift, or whether expectations need adjustment. It encourages us to remain open to new perspectives, to stay self-aware, and to communicate honestly with those we trust.

Trust with doubt is responsive; it has the capacity to grow deeper or to scale back as circumstances require. Rather than confining us to one level of trust, it allows us to adapt, to strengthen bonds, or to establish distance if necessary. By making trust a fluid, evolving process, doubt enables us to create relationships that can stand the test of time and circumstance. **This form of trust is resilient, capable of enduring misunderstandings, disappointments, and life's inevitable changes without collapsing under their weight.**

For example, in friendships, doubt allows us to reassess the relationship when life circumstances change. We may find ourselves spending less time with a friend due to new work or family commitments, and doubt may prompt us to check in, realign our expectations, and continue supporting each other in ways that reflect our current realities. This ability to re-evaluate trust prevents us from feeling obligated or constrained by the past, allowing us to embrace each relationship as it is, rather than as it once was.

Sustaining Trust in a Morally Ambiguous World

In this sense, doubt doesn't limit trust—it **sustains it**. It provides the realism that allows trust to thrive even in morally ambiguous settings. In a world where ethical clarity is often in short supply, trust that incorporates doubt doesn't rely on rigid ideals; instead, it adapts to the reality of human imperfection. By approaching trust with caution and flexibility, we avoid the heartbreak and disillusionment that often accompany blind faith. **We enjoy the richness of genuine connection without sacrificing our discernment or security.**

Doubt ensures that trust remains a **conscious, intentional choice** rather than an automatic expectation. It reminds us to maintain clarity in our expectations, to communicate openly about boundaries, and to engage in relationships that honor our values. Doubt, in this way, is not a lack of trust but an expression of wisdom—a recognition that trust, like all things valuable, requires nurturing, vigilance, and respect for the complexities of human relationships.

By welcoming doubt as a core element of trust, we build connections that are both authentic and resilient, able to withstand the pressures of an imperfect world. We create partnerships, friendships, and commitments that grow in depth over time, grounded in mutual respect and sustained by an ongoing commitment to accountability, honesty, and integrity.

Trust with doubt becomes a source of strength, allowing us to approach relationships with open-heartedness yet retaining our autonomy and discernment. In an unpredictable world, trust sustained by doubt allows us to remain open, compassionate, and engaged without feeling unprotected or naive. It is a trust that offers freedom rather than restriction, a trust that encourages growth, connection, and understanding.

In a world where human behavior can be unpredictable and ethical standards uncertain, trust with doubt becomes our best way forward. It enables us to create bonds that are real, relationships that can endure, and communities that are built on the honest recognition of our shared human experience. This balanced trust—one that sees doubt not as an adversary but as a guide—is the kind of trust that not only survives but thrives in a complex, ever-changing world.

The New Foundation of Trust: Built on Awareness and Choice

As we move through this book, consider how this reimagined model of trust might apply in your own life. Think of situations where traditional trust—trust that assumes unwavering confidence without question—feels too risky or too limiting. Imagine how introducing doubt might reshape that trust, making it feel safer, stronger, and more adaptable. By allowing doubt to guide us, we can create trust that is grounded in reality, a trust that's capable of adjusting to change without breaking.

This redefined approach invites us to see **trust as a conscious choice rather than a passive expectation**. Instead of simply deciding to trust or not to trust, we can incorporate doubt as a guiding force, one that encourages us to set boundaries, demand accountability, and allow trust to grow gradually rather than all at once. This method isn't about holding back affection, cooperation, or confidence; rather, it's about nurturing trust in a way that respects our need for clarity and protection. By doing so, we can avoid the pitfalls of blind faith and reduce the likelihood of disillusionment or betrayal.

Trust as a Balanced Art of Awareness and Flexibility

In this new view, trust is no longer a leap of faith; it is **an art of balance**. It requires awareness and careful attention, a sense of openness paired with discernment. This balance allows trust to be grounded in the present, capable of adapting to new information and responsive to the changing dynamics of relationships. Trust is not a static state; it is fluid and responsive, able to expand or contract as circumstances require. This flexibility does not weaken trust; instead, it gives trust depth, making it both realistic and resilient.

Doubt doesn't weaken trust; it gives it depth. When doubt is present, trust becomes more than just an ideal—it becomes a practical, adaptable foundation that is capable of surviving life's natural ups and downs. It allows us to remain open to the world's possibilities without compromising our sense of protection. By practicing trust with doubt, we create a foundation that is not only enduring but also capable of growth, a foundation that can support us through the complexities and uncertainties of the world we live in.

This balanced trust allows us to cultivate relationships and connections that are **rich yet sustainable**. We're able to trust fully while staying grounded, to engage with others while keeping a sense of our own boundaries. This form of trust recognizes that perfection is not a prerequisite; instead, it emphasizes honesty, accountability, and a shared commitment to growth. By making trust adaptable, we ensure that it can be strengthened over time, even as circumstances shift and evolve.

Exploring Trust as a Process Across Different Settings

This chapter serves as the cornerstone of a new approach to trust—an approach that invites us to examine **how to build balanced trust across all areas of our lives**. As we continue, we will explore how to apply this balanced, resilient form of trust in various settings: in the workplace, in friendships, in romantic relationships, and within communities. We will look at practical ways to incorporate doubt in each context, using it as a means to establish boundaries, set expectations, and cultivate genuine connections that are built on mutual respect and understanding.

In the workplace, for instance, this approach may mean creating transparent accountability structures, fostering a culture of open communication, and encouraging teamwork while acknowledging individual boundaries. In friendships, balanced trust might look like respecting personal limits, allowing relationships to grow at a natural pace, and being open to honest discussions about expectations. In romantic relationships, it could mean practicing open dialogue, setting shared goals, and checking in periodically to ensure that both partners feel safe and supported.

By viewing trust as a **process rather than a destination**, we allow it to be adaptable to each relationship and each setting. This flexible approach makes it possible for us to trust without feeling vulnerable, to be open without losing our sense of security, and to create connections that are both meaningful and stable.

Building Trust That Honors Ethical Ambiguities and Complex Motivations

In a world where ethics are often ambiguous and motivations aren't always transparent, **trust supported by doubt isn't just an option—it's essential**. Blind trust, while idealistic, often fails to hold up in situations where values and motivations are in flux. Trust built on awareness and choice, however, enables us to navigate these complexities with confidence and clarity. We recognize that people may have a mix of motivations, that ethical choices aren't always straightforward, and that even good intentions can sometimes fall short. By integrating doubt, we accept these realities and build a trust that can withstand them.

This new foundation of trust empowers us to engage in relationships and commitments with a full awareness of their inherent complexities. We are not asking others to be flawless; instead, we are asking for accountability, honesty, and a commitment to shared values. This balanced approach to trust allows us to create relationships that respect both our ideals and our realities, fostering a sense of integrity and alignment even in a morally complex world.

Practical Tools for Developing Trust with Depth

In the chapters that follow, we'll explore practical tools and strategies for cultivating this balanced, adaptable form of trust. We'll look at **methods for setting boundaries**, **techniques for establishing accountability**, and

approaches to managing expectations. These tools are designed to help you incorporate doubt constructively, turning it into a resource for growth rather than a source of hesitation or fear. Through reflective exercises, self-assessment tools, and real-life case studies, you'll learn how to make trust an intentional choice—one that aligns with your values, respects your needs, and supports your personal and professional relationships.

For instance, we'll look at ways to conduct trust "check-ins" in relationships, to establish clear expectations in work collaborations, and to navigate trust in community settings where motivations and goals may vary widely. By applying these tools, you'll be able to create a **balanced foundation of trust** that enhances your interactions and connections while protecting your sense of self and security.

Embracing Trust as a Dynamic Force in Our Lives

Ultimately, this redefined trust—one built on awareness and choice—is a **dynamic force** in our lives. It encourages us to remain open to others without losing sight of our own boundaries, to believe in others' potential without ignoring the need for accountability. It allows us to enjoy the beauty of human connection while honoring our need for clarity, balance, and security.

As you read through each chapter, consider how you might bring this balanced trust into your own relationships, whether with friends, family, colleagues, or within larger communities. Ask yourself how doubt can serve as a tool for discernment and strength, allowing you to trust more fully and effectively. Imagine how this trust can transform your interactions, offering you a sense of confidence and peace that comes from knowing your trust is placed with intention, not assumption.

This new foundation of trust is about engaging with life fully yet wisely, about embracing both connection and independence. It invites you to participate in the world openly, knowing that trust doesn't require perfection but rather **a commitment to growth, accountability, and honesty**. In a world where change is constant and certainty rare, this flexible, intentional approach to trust gives us a path forward—a way to create connections that are meaningful, ethical, and lasting.

As we embark on this journey together, may this new foundation of trust guide you, offering a balance between the heart's desire to connect and the mind's need for discernment.

2: The Mechanics of Trust and Doubt in an Unethical Landscape

In an ideal world, trust might be straightforward—a natural bond formed through honesty and shared values. Yet, in an increasingly complex and ethically ambiguous landscape, trust is anything but simple. It requires careful navigation, especially when the lines between right and wrong blur. Doubt, often seen as a barrier, becomes a guiding force in such environments, helping us assess intentions, verify actions, and protect our boundaries. This chapter delves into the mechanics of how trust and doubt coexist, offering a framework to engage thoughtfully in relationships and decisions where ethics may be uncertain or compromised.

The Role of Doubt as a Filter for Trust in an Ethically Compromised World

In an ideal world, trust might be straightforward, a natural state we offer to those around us. We'd believe in people's intentions, count on organizations to act in our best interests, and expect systems to function transparently. Trust would be based on an assumption of shared values, mutual respect, and a commitment to integrity. In such a world, trusting others would feel intuitive, requiring little hesitation or concern. We'd extend trust freely, knowing that those we trusted were as committed to honesty and responsibility as we were.

However, in today's complex and often ethically compromised landscape, trust has become more nuanced. The layers of ambiguity in people's motivations, the mixed interests of organizations, and the blurred boundaries in our systems make it increasingly challenging to offer trust without question. **Doubt, once seen as the enemy of trust, has emerged as a crucial ally**, helping us navigate an environment where intentions are often concealed, where integrity cannot be taken for granted, and where transparency is not always present.

Doubt acts as a filter, allowing us to sift through intentions, claims, and actions, giving us a way to engage meaningfully without becoming overly vulnerable. It's a tool that lets us examine the reliability of others while protecting our boundaries, ideals, and values. In ethically ambiguous settings, doubt encourages us to **approach trust selectively**, assessing each relationship, commitment, or decision with care. This doesn't mean that doubt replaces trust; rather, it enables a smarter, more informed kind of trust, one that is backed by awareness and discernment.

Trust in a World of Complex Motives: Why Doubt is Essential

Today, we navigate a world where institutions, leaders, and even personal connections can have motives that are layered and complex. Organizations, for example, often face competing interests—profit motives versus social responsibility, shareholder demands versus customer trust, or regulatory compliance versus innovation. This complexity can lead to situations where what appears trustworthy on the surface may not hold up upon closer examination. When we introduce doubt as a filter in these contexts, **we are not being cynical; we are being realistic**. Doubt allows us to protect ourselves from putting blind faith in entities that may have conflicting interests or motivations.

In this ethically ambiguous environment, **doubt becomes a protective measure**. It empowers us to look beyond appearances, to question and probe, ensuring that the individuals and systems we trust are deserving of that trust. Doubt prompts us to ask questions, to demand transparency, and to establish accountability as prerequisites for trust. Rather than relying on assumptions or societal expectations, we allow doubt to guide us toward a form of trust that is intentional and grounded in reality.

For example, in professional or institutional contexts, doubt encourages us to verify credentials, request references, and investigate reputations before entering partnerships. When choosing to work with a new organization, doubt prompts us to explore its past behavior, examining its ethics, reliability, and history. This due diligence isn't a sign of mistrust; it's a commitment to establishing a **foundation for responsible trust**. By incorporating doubt, we're able to engage with others confidently, knowing that we're basing our trust on observable evidence rather than wishful thinking.

The Mechanics of Doubt as a Trust Filter: Discernment and Protection

Doubt functions as a **filter by allowing us to discern** between those who are trustworthy and those who may not be, between claims that are legitimate and those that may be misleading, and between actions that align with our values and those that compromise them. This discernment is crucial in today's world, where trust often involves risk, and where misplaced trust can lead to significant consequences. Doubt gives us a way to calibrate our trust, guiding us to extend it carefully rather than recklessly.

This filtering process prevents us from automatically placing trust in individuals, systems, or institutions that may not deserve it. **It gives us a level of control over our trust** by allowing us to engage thoughtfully, reducing the likelihood of disappointment or betrayal. In this sense, doubt doesn't close us off from trusting others; it directs our trust wisely, ensuring that it is based on actions and evidence rather than assumptions.

Through the lens of doubt, trust becomes **a conscious, measured decision** rather than an automatic response. It encourages us to look for consistency in behavior, alignment with values, and transparency in communication. It allows us to trust, but with open eyes, balancing our natural inclination to connect with our responsibility to protect our values, goals, and well-being. By integrating doubt as a filter, we ensure that our trust remains a reflection of our ideals rather than a vulnerability that others could exploit.

Real-World Application: Trusting with Doubt as a Guide

Consider a situation where a company, known for questionable practices in the past, offers you a business partnership. The company's representatives present their vision confidently, emphasizing the potential for mutual growth and success. Without doubt as a filter, you might accept their proposal at face value, viewing the partnership as a promising opportunity. This would be an example of **blind trust**—the assumption that the company's intentions align perfectly with your own.

But **with doubt as a guiding force**, you approach the offer with a healthy level of skepticism, examining the company's past behavior, considering its reputation in the industry, and evaluating whether its goals align with your values. This doesn't mean you're cynical or unwilling to work with them—it simply means that you are assessing, verifying, and ensuring that your trust, if extended, will be placed with awareness. **Doubt becomes a tool of discernment**, prompting you to seek out evidence that validates the company's claims.

In this scenario, doubt guides you to set conditions, to communicate openly about your expectations, and to proceed with caution rather than reckless optimism. Perhaps you request transparency in financial reporting, or you set up periodic reviews to monitor the partnership's progress. These actions don't indicate a lack of trust; they reflect a commitment to **building a trust that is supported by accountability and transparency**. By allowing doubt to influence your decision-making, you engage in the partnership responsibly, maintaining both trust and protection.

Doubt as a Pathway to Empowerment and Realism

In ethically compromised environments, doubt also empowers us to remain realistic, giving us a way to engage meaningfully without lowering our standards or boundaries. **Doubt reminds us that not everyone has our best interests at heart**, and that not every system operates with integrity. This knowledge doesn't make us pessimistic; it makes us informed, allowing us to make choices that align with our values. Doubt serves as a reminder that we can participate in relationships, organizations, and commitments without compromising our ideals.

For instance, in situations where we are asked to support an organization or movement, doubt encourages us to dig deeper, to question motivations, and to ensure that our trust aligns with our values. By allowing doubt to guide our engagement, we are empowered to act consciously, contributing to causes that genuinely reflect our beliefs. This practice of **selective trust** helps us avoid the trap of endorsing or supporting entities that may ultimately misalign with our values.

In this way, doubt doesn't restrict us from trusting others; it simply directs us to trust with awareness. It allows us to establish boundaries, to engage thoughtfully, and to remain true to ourselves in environments where ethical compromises are common. This approach to trust, shaped by doubt, gives us the freedom to participate fully without feeling vulnerable to disillusionment or regret.

Doubt as a Framework for Ethical Engagement

Through the lens of doubt, we gain the tools needed to **engage ethically and responsibly**. We're not simply trusting others to uphold standards—we're actively verifying, questioning, and aligning our choices with our own ideals. This process of filtered trust can be applied in any setting, whether we're forming new friendships, entering professional partnerships, or supporting larger causes. Doubt allows us to engage meaningfully without losing sight of our own ethical boundaries, and it offers us a framework for **sustainable, ethical trust**.

As we move forward in this book, consider how doubt might serve as a framework in your own life. Let it be a reminder that trust is not an all-or-nothing state; it is a dynamic choice, one that we shape through discernment, reflection, and a commitment to integrity. By trusting with doubt, we create relationships, partnerships, and commitments that are both meaningful and resilient, capable of thriving even in an ethically compromised world.

The Psychological and Philosophical Foundations of Trust and Doubt

To understand why doubt can be a powerful partner to trust, it helps to explore the **psychological and philosophical roots** of these concepts. Psychologically, trust is often seen as a natural inclination, something that enables us to bond with others, form communities, and find security in relationships. Trust creates a sense of predictability, allowing us to rely on others and to reduce our own need for constant vigilance. It provides us with stability and enables us to focus our energy on shared goals and cooperative pursuits. From an early age, we learn that trust is essential for survival and connection—babies instinctively trust their caregivers, for example, because their survival depends on it.

As we grow, this **early trust forms the basis for social bonds** that enable us to thrive within families, friendships, and societies. Psychologists argue that trust is rooted in our need for attachment and belonging, as it allows us to feel safe in our social environments. Trust reduces anxiety, fostering a sense of security that enables us to take risks, form deeper connections, and collaborate meaningfully. This trust is reinforced through our life experiences; we learn to expect that people and systems will often, though not always, be there for us in predictable ways.

However, the world we encounter as adults is far more complex. We become aware of competing interests, diverse ethical beliefs, and a spectrum of motivations that may not always align with our own. Relationships and institutions are layered with intricacies, and trust, once automatic, now demands a level of discernment. We recognize that **blind trust can be risky**, that people and systems are fallible, and that motivations are often complex. This shift from childlike trust to an adult understanding of its complexities requires us to reassess and redefine trust as something dynamic and conditional, rather than absolute.

Doubt, on the other hand, is often regarded as an evolutionary adaptation, a response to the need for caution in an unpredictable environment. While trust allows us to connect, doubt allows us to protect ourselves. Doubt helps us question, reassess, and guard against potential harm. Psychologically, doubt serves as a cognitive tool that enables us to consider alternative possibilities, pause to evaluate information, and weigh risks and benefits. This ability to question our environment empowers us to make informed choices rather than relying solely on hope or assumption.

Doubt, therefore, has been essential for our survival as a species. It allows us to evaluate situations and people, ensuring that we don't expose ourselves to unnecessary risks. While trust fosters **connection and cooperation, doubt fosters discernment and protection**. Together, they create a balanced framework for navigating complex, morally ambiguous landscapes. This balance enables us to maintain meaningful relationships and partnerships while preserving our sense of safety and autonomy.

Doubt as a Foundation for Wisdom and Critical Thinking

Philosophically, doubt has long been celebrated as a cornerstone of wisdom and a pathway to deeper understanding. For centuries, thinkers have argued that doubt is not only useful but essential to the pursuit of truth and knowledge. **Socrates, often regarded as the father of Western philosophy, argued that doubt was the beginning of wisdom**. By questioning assumptions, he believed that we could dismantle false beliefs and uncover more profound truths. Socratic questioning—the process of continuously asking questions to challenge established ideas—remains a foundational method for developing critical thinking skills today.

From a philosophical perspective, doubt is not a sign of mistrust but of a **higher commitment to understanding and truth**. It signifies a willingness to look beyond appearances and seek a deeper reality. This philosophical embrace of doubt positions it not as a roadblock to trust but as a tool that enhances it. When we approach trust with doubt, we're essentially saying that we value integrity and truth enough to seek confirmation rather than accepting things at face value.

In the context of trust, doubt allows us to **test and verify**. Rather than undermining trust, doubt ensures that our trust is built on a foundation of reliability and integrity rather than assumption. It encourages us to seek consistency in others' actions, to ask for transparency, and to validate claims, thereby strengthening our ability to rely on them. Philosophically, doubt can be viewed as a process of refining trust, ensuring that it is earned and deserved. This approach shifts trust from being a naive assumption to being an **intentional, well-considered choice**.

Doubt as a Protective Mechanism in an Ethically Compromised World

In a world where ethical integrity is not always a given, this foundation of trust supported by doubt is essential. Doubt acts as a **protective mechanism**, helping us assess whether our trust is well-placed. If we find that our trust was misplaced, doubt allows us to adjust our expectations, reset boundaries, and make necessary changes without feeling destabilized or betrayed. By incorporating doubt, we maintain our ability to trust others while preserving our clarity and self-protection. Doubt enables us to stay connected to others and to engage in meaningful relationships, all while honoring our boundaries and ideals.

Imagine a scenario where you're considering a partnership with someone whose values don't fully align with yours. Doubt prompts you to ask questions, set conditions, and test the waters before fully committing. In doing so, you're not acting out of cynicism but out of **commitment to preserving your own ethical standards**. By allowing doubt to shape your approach, you protect yourself from aligning with values that don't resonate with you while still remaining open to connection and collaboration.

In personal relationships, doubt allows us to **pace our trust**. We can give others the benefit of the doubt while being mindful of signs that might suggest caution. This approach helps us build resilient relationships that can withstand misunderstandings, disagreements, and even occasional disappointments. Doubt gives us the flexibility to reevaluate, ensuring that trust is based on observed behavior rather than idealized assumptions.

In institutions, doubt encourages us to seek transparency and accountability. In a world where corporate scandals, political corruption, and social injustice are all too common, doubt allows us to remain vigilant, questioning motives and demanding ethical practices. By doing so, we uphold the principles of trust in a way that's grounded in responsibility. We trust only what has proven trustworthy, ensuring that our confidence is placed with care.

The Harmony of Trust and Doubt: A Balanced Framework

Together, **trust and doubt create a balanced framework** for navigating an ethically ambiguous world. Trust allows us to connect, cooperate, and move forward with optimism, while doubt enables us to discern, protect, and make choices aligned with our values. Trust and doubt, when integrated, prevent us from becoming either overly naive or overly skeptical. Instead, they empower us to approach relationships, commitments, and institutions with clarity, awareness, and strength.

When trust and doubt are balanced, we gain the freedom to **engage openly without losing our autonomy**. We can work with others, enter into agreements, and share in collective efforts while maintaining a sense of self-protection and integrity. This harmony between trust and doubt encourages us to trust not blindly but wisely, to remain open to others while honoring our boundaries and ideals.

Doubt, therefore, isn't an obstacle to trust but a complement to it, adding depth and durability to the relationships and commitments we choose to engage in. In an ethically compromised world, this balance is crucial, as it allows us to foster connections and collaborations that are resilient, ethical, and aligned with our personal values. By approaching trust as a process that is refined through doubt, we are able to create connections that are both meaningful and secure.

As we continue to explore the nature of trust and doubt, consider how these psychological and philosophical foundations might influence your own approach to relationships, commitments, and values. Embracing doubt not as a barrier but as a guide allows us to trust responsibly, empowering us to engage in life with a sense of purpose, authenticity, and ethical clarity.

How Doubt Supports Trust in Unreliable Environments

In environments where trustworthiness is uncertain, doubt serves as an invaluable tool, allowing us to **engage carefully and responsibly**. In an ideal world, trust might be a straightforward leap of faith, but in situations where people, institutions, or systems have shown inconsistency or questionable ethics, doubt becomes essential. It encourages us to approach trust deliberately, to seek verification, to ask for transparency, and to establish accountability. By doing so, doubt transforms trust from a passive expectation into an active process, one that we build upon concrete, observable actions.

When we practice trust in unreliable environments, doubt plays a guiding role, helping us to set **boundaries, conditions, and checkpoints**. Instead of simply hoping for the best, we're prompted to build trust incrementally, based on evidence of integrity, reliability, and consistency. This approach doesn't mean that we assume everyone is untrustworthy; rather, it reflects a commitment to ensuring that our trust is placed wisely, with the awareness that not all people or systems meet our standards. Through doubt, trust becomes

a dynamic exchange, where both parties contribute to creating a relationship that's respectful, transparent, and mutually responsible.

Doubt as a Tool for Discernment in the World of Social Media

Consider the world of social media, where information flows rapidly, but not always accurately. Misinformation, fake news, and sensationalism are common, making it challenging to determine what is real, trustworthy, and relevant. In this setting, **doubt serves as a critical filter**, helping us navigate an environment that thrives on speed and often overlooks accuracy. By prompting us to question the credibility of sources, cross-check facts, and withhold judgment until we've gathered sufficient evidence, doubt enables us to sift through the noise and find reliable voices.

For instance, when we see a piece of news on social media, doubt may prompt us to ask questions like, "Who published this? Is it a credible source? Are other reputable outlets reporting the same information?" Doubt encourages us to avoid quick reactions and instead to **seek confirmation from multiple sources**, ensuring that the information we act upon is as accurate as possible. By doubting selectively, we don't lose faith in our ability to connect, learn, and find value in social media; instead, we become discerning consumers of information, able to differentiate between sources that have proven reliable over time and those that may be driven by agendas, misinformation, or bias.

Doubt also allows us to avoid **polarizing debates** or emotionally charged content that may not be based in fact. It enables us to approach social media with a critical mindset, reducing the likelihood of spreading misinformation or forming opinions based on incomplete information. In a digital world where trust is easily manipulated, doubt helps us maintain control over our beliefs and actions, ensuring that our interactions remain rooted in reality and integrity.

Doubt as a Framework for Accountability in Professional Settings

In professional environments, **doubt plays an equally vital role in fostering trust**, especially when working with new clients, partners, or suppliers whose practices and ethics we may be unfamiliar with. In such situations, doubt encourages us to take a proactive stance, asking questions, setting expectations, and creating conditions that ensure accountability. For instance, when collaborating with a new client, rather than assuming they will uphold the same standards we hold ourselves to, doubt prompts us to **communicate expectations clearly** and establish terms that reinforce those standards.

Doubt may lead us to review contracts carefully, to outline deliverables and timelines explicitly, and to conduct periodic evaluations to ensure that both parties are meeting their commitments. This doesn't imply mistrust; rather, it reflects a commitment to **establishing a foundation of reliability**. When both parties know that actions will be monitored and that trust will be reinforced through consistency, they are more likely to approach the partnership with transparency, respect, and responsibility.

Doubt, in this way, becomes a mechanism that strengthens the professional relationship. It ensures that neither side takes the other's trust for granted and that both are held to clear, mutually agreed-upon standards. In uncertain conditions, where motivations may not be fully transparent or where stakes are high, doubt provides a structure that allows trust to grow through **repeated actions and verifiable commitments**. The result is a relationship grounded in realistic expectations, one that can withstand challenges because it is built on a framework of accountability and respect.

Building Trust Gradually: The Power of Doubt in High-Stakes Environments

In high-stakes environments, where the consequences of misplaced trust can be significant, doubt serves as a **protective layer** that helps us pace the growth of trust carefully. For example, in industries like finance, healthcare, or law, where the impact of trust is substantial, doubt allows us to engage responsibly by seeking transparency and verification. In healthcare, doubt may encourage a patient to seek a second opinion, not because they mistrust their doctor but because they recognize the importance of getting multiple perspectives to ensure the best possible outcome. In finance, doubt might prompt an investor to review a company's financial records or past performance before committing funds.

Doubt in these contexts ensures that trust is **built gradually, reinforced by observable actions**. Rather than diving in with blind confidence, individuals take time to verify, assess, and build trust incrementally. By introducing doubt as a guide, they protect themselves from unnecessary risks while allowing trust to grow in a way that feels secure and sustainable. This approach to trust acknowledges the complexities of high-stakes decisions and allows individuals to make informed choices based on a combination of faith and fact.

Creating a Culture of Transparency and Reliability through Doubt

Doubt also fosters a culture of **transparency and reliability** by encouraging open communication and accountability. When doubt is present, we are more likely to ask questions, to set boundaries, and to require that commitments be upheld with integrity. In team environments, doubt allows us to establish norms that prioritize honesty and follow-through, creating a space where people feel responsible for their actions and motivated to build trust over time. This culture of accountability is essential in unreliable environments, as it ensures that trust is not assumed but earned through consistent, reliable behavior.

For instance, a manager who uses doubt as a framework might regularly check in with their team, asking for progress updates, reviewing goals, and providing feedback. This doesn't mean the manager distrusts their team; rather, they are creating a structure in which trust can be reinforced through **transparency and communication**. When team members know that their work will be reviewed and that expectations are clear, they are more likely to approach their tasks with responsibility and dedication. This approach not only builds trust within the team but also empowers team members to feel confident in their roles, knowing that their efforts are aligned with clearly defined standards.

In organizational settings, doubt can lead to the implementation of **systems that promote ethical practices**. For example, a company might establish regular audits, compliance checks, or open-door policies that encourage employees to report concerns. These practices create a culture where trust is backed by verification, allowing both employees and leaders to feel secure in their interactions. By integrating doubt into the structure of the organization, companies can build a foundation of trust that is resilient to challenges and rooted in accountability.

Doubt as a Mechanism for Realistic and Sustainable Trust

When doubt supports trust, it creates a foundation that is both **realistic and sustainable**. In uncertain environments, doubt encourages us to take proactive steps that protect our interests while allowing us to remain open to trust. Rather than leaving ourselves vulnerable to potential disappointments, we approach trust with a mindset of discernment, one that values consistency and reliability over assumption. This realistic approach enables us to build relationships and partnerships that can withstand the tests of time and change, as they are grounded in shared responsibility.

This sustainable model of trust is particularly valuable in situations where ethical standards may be ambiguous or where past experiences have shown that trust alone is insufficient. For instance, someone who has been let down in past friendships or relationships may use doubt as a means of protecting their heart, allowing trust to develop gradually based on mutual effort and respect. This doesn't imply cynicism; it reflects a commitment to building trust in a way that honors both parties' needs and boundaries.

Doubt, then, does not restrict trust but **enriches it** by making it adaptable, responsive, and durable. When we integrate doubt, trust is no longer a leap of faith but an evolving commitment, one that grows and strengthens as we witness reliability and integrity over time. This balanced trust is not easily shaken by setbacks because it is grounded in the reality of human imperfection and the complexity of modern environments. Doubt allows us to trust deeply and meaningfully without feeling exposed to unnecessary risks, creating a model of trust that is both heartfelt and wise.

As we continue exploring the interplay between trust and doubt, consider how these principles might apply to your own life, particularly in environments where reliability may be uncertain. Allow doubt to guide you in asking the right questions, setting boundaries, and establishing accountability, all while remaining open to the potential for connection, collaboration, and mutual respect. By approaching trust through the lens of doubt, we not only protect ourselves but also foster relationships, teams, and communities that are grounded in integrity and empowered to thrive.

Real-Life Examples of Trust Supported by Doubt in Challenging Situations

Real-life examples show us that **doubt can be a powerful ally** in building trust, especially in challenging or ethically ambiguous situations. Below, we explore several cases where individuals and organizations have effectively used doubt as a constructive force to create sustainable and resilient trust.

Case Study: Trust in Journalism

In journalism, where ethical integrity is paramount, doubt serves as a **cornerstone for credibility**. Investigative journalists, for instance, are trained to approach every claim with a level of skepticism, rigorously verifying information from multiple sources before publishing. This doubt-driven approach is not about mistrust; it's about a commitment to accuracy, accountability, and public trust. By questioning every piece of information, journalists build trust with their audience, demonstrating a **dedication to truth and transparency**.

This methodical, doubt-centered approach safeguards the journalist from spreading misinformation while reinforcing the public's trust in the publication. The process ensures that readers can rely on the news source, knowing that it upholds high standards of fact-checking and unbiased reporting. In an era where misinformation is rampant, **doubt acts as a filter** that helps audiences discern reputable sources from unreliable ones.

For example, during global crises, reputable news organizations meticulously vet information before release, often conducting on-the-ground fact-checks, sourcing from independent witnesses, and corroborating with other reliable agencies. Readers who see this commitment to rigorous standards are more likely to place trust in that publication, knowing their trust is **backed by accountability and diligence** rather than blind acceptance. In this way, doubt not only protects the integrity of journalism but fosters a lasting relationship of trust with the public.

Case Study: Doubt in International Business

In international business, trust across cultures and regulatory environments is both **essential and complex.** Imagine a company that wants to partner with a foreign organization in a country where business practices differ significantly. Rather than diving into the partnership with blind confidence, the company uses doubt as a constructive tool. It requests transparency around financial records, verifies compliance with international standards, and builds in checkpoints to evaluate ethical practices over time.

This doubt-driven approach doesn't hinder the partnership; instead, it strengthens it by creating a structure of **accountability and mutual respect**. Both companies understand that trust is contingent upon demonstrated reliability, and this understanding builds a relationship resilient to the challenges of cross-cultural and cross-regulatory partnerships.

For example, in joint ventures between Western and Asian companies, differences in legal frameworks and ethical norms often surface. A doubt-centered approach leads both sides to establish frequent reporting, compliance checks, and transparent communication to align expectations. Knowing that their actions are subject to verification incentivizes the foreign organization to uphold ethical standards, thereby **creating a partnership grounded in transparency and trust**. This careful approach avoids misunderstandings and fosters a relationship built on clear communication and shared expectations.

Case Study: Doubt in Personal Relationships

In personal relationships, doubt plays a valuable role, especially for individuals who have experienced betrayal or a **loss of trust** in the past. For instance, consider someone who has been hurt by a close friend. When they begin building new friendships, doubt might prompt them to set boundaries, take things slowly, and allow trust to develop gradually. This isn't about holding a grudge; it's about **protecting themselves while staying open to connection**.

Doubt guides them to observe behaviors over time, allowing them to evaluate whether their new friend respects boundaries, shows consistency, and upholds values aligned with their own. By pacing trust in this way, doubt serves as a **healing mechanism**, helping them approach relationships with discernment. Over time, as the new friend demonstrates reliability, doubt naturally diminishes, replaced by a trust that is both deep and resilient.

This gradual approach not only helps the individual regain confidence in others but ensures that the trust they offer is realistic and sustainable. Rather than feeling vulnerable to past hurts, they can trust again without compromising their emotional safety. Doubt, in this context, **enables a healthier approach to trust**, allowing them to engage fully while honoring their boundaries and emotional needs.

Case Study: Doubt in Healthcare

In healthcare, patients often place enormous trust in medical professionals, sometimes at the expense of their own intuition or judgment. However, when patients or family members introduce doubt—by seeking second opinions, asking questions, or requesting additional information—they are not displaying mistrust but instead are ensuring that their trust is well-placed. **Doubt in this setting becomes a tool for clarity**, helping both patients and doctors align on expectations and work toward the best outcomes.

For instance, a patient facing a serious diagnosis might seek a second opinion to confirm the initial assessment, ask for explanations on treatment options, or research potential side effects. This doesn't mean the patient mistrusts the doctor but rather that they are taking an active role in their care, ensuring they understand the process fully. Doubt empowers patients to verify information, clarify misunderstandings, and feel more confident about their medical choices.

In healthcare systems where policies encourage patients to ask questions and verify information, satisfaction and trust levels are often higher. Patients feel **empowered to engage** with their care, knowing that their trust is grounded in a collaborative approach rather than blind faith. This creates a healthcare experience that is both compassionate and transparent, fostering a relationship built on mutual understanding and respect.

In medical practices, open communication channels—such as patient access to medical records, detailed consultations, and clear consent forms—further reinforce trust. Patients can rest assured that they are making informed decisions, leading to better compliance and a stronger bond between doctor and patient. Doubt, when embraced in healthcare, **fosters a transparent and respectful relationship**, allowing patients to feel safe and valued in their care journey.

Case Study: Doubt in Education and Academic Integrity

In education, particularly in research and academia, doubt is a critical element of maintaining **academic integrity** and building trust among peers, students, and the public. Professors, scientists, and students are encouraged to approach knowledge with a healthy level of skepticism, to verify data, and to critically evaluate findings. In academic publishing, peer review processes rely heavily on doubt to assess the validity of research before it reaches a wider audience.

For example, a researcher who presents groundbreaking findings must submit their work to a **peer review process**, where other experts in the field scrutinize the methods, data, and conclusions. This process isn't a display of mistrust but a commitment to ensuring the research is accurate, replicable, and reliable. By introducing doubt in this manner, academia upholds high standards, ensuring that published research is credible and trustworthy.

Moreover, educational institutions often encourage students to **question assumptions and explore multiple perspectives** as part of their learning journey. This academic practice reinforces the idea that doubt is a path to deeper understanding, not a barrier to knowledge. Students learn that it's acceptable—and even encouraged—to question established theories and to seek evidence to support their viewpoints. Doubt, in this context, **fosters intellectual honesty and critical thinking** skills, preparing students to engage with complex information responsibly.

The use of doubt in academia ultimately builds trust in educational and research institutions, as the public sees that knowledge is not accepted blindly but subjected to rigorous scrutiny. This trust is foundational in fields like medicine, engineering, and social sciences, where academic integrity directly impacts public well-being. By establishing doubt as a central component of the academic process, institutions ensure that trust in education and research is both resilient and deserved.

The Common Thread: Building Trust through Accountability

and Transparency

Across these diverse examples, we see a common thread: **doubt is not an impediment to trust but a pathway to strengthening it**. Whether in journalism, international business, personal relationships, healthcare, or academia, doubt encourages accountability, transparency, and consistent demonstration of integrity. It creates a framework where trust is built on a foundation of responsibility, rather than on passive acceptance.

By actively verifying actions, requiring transparency, and setting standards of accountability, doubt **transforms trust into an ongoing commitment**. This approach not only protects individuals and institutions from the risks of misplaced trust but also fosters relationships that are resilient, adaptable, and grounded in mutual respect.

In an ethically ambiguous world, doubt enables us to navigate challenges thoughtfully, creating relationships, partnerships, and communities where trust is nurtured responsibly. It allows us to engage meaningfully with others while maintaining a sense of protection, clarity, and purpose.

Creating a Foundation for Trust in an Unethical Landscape

As the previous examples demonstrate, **doubt doesn't destroy trust**; rather, it fortifies it by adding layers of reality, accountability, and transparency. In a world where ethics can be compromised, where intentions may be unclear, and where reliability is often uncertain, doubt serves as a crucial mechanism that allows trust to function effectively. Instead of accepting everything at face value, doubt gives us **the tools to build relationships, partnerships, and commitments** that are honest, respectful, and aligned with our values. This approach to trust ensures that we engage with others meaningfully, while safeguarding our integrity.

In today's complex landscape, doubt acts as a **buffer against naivety**, reminding us to remain vigilant and to confirm before committing. It allows us to differentiate between people and institutions that are genuinely aligned with our values and those that may not be. Through doubt, we are empowered to create a version of trust that is **thoughtful and intentional**, a trust that is earned and reinforced through consistency, honesty, and integrity.

The Role of Doubt in Building Resilient Trust

By incorporating doubt into our approach to trust, we're not closing ourselves off from the world. Instead, we're **creating a foundation for trust that is grounded in wisdom and resilience**. This trust is adaptable to change, capable of overcoming uncertainty, and designed to thrive in the face of complexity. It is not a passive, one-time choice but an ongoing process, a relationship that grows deeper as it's continually reinforced by reliable actions.

In an unethical landscape, trust built on doubt becomes a proactive process rather than a blind leap of faith. Doubt encourages us to ask questions, establish boundaries, and require verification in situations where motivations may be ambiguous. For instance, in personal relationships, we may choose to trust gradually, observing patterns of behavior over time to ensure consistency. In professional settings, we may establish clear expectations and accountability measures, allowing trust to grow as each party demonstrates reliability. **Doubt here acts as the silent guardian of trust**, helping us avoid the pitfalls of misplaced confidence while allowing trust to flourish where it's truly deserved.

Consider the difference between blind trust and trust that's informed by doubt. Blind trust assumes that others will act ethically simply because we expect them to. But trust informed by doubt recognizes that not everyone will share our values or motivations. It gives us the clarity to engage selectively, extending trust only to those who demonstrate trustworthiness. In this way, doubt doesn't hinder connection; it empowers us to form bonds that are both meaningful and resilient.

Building Relationships Aligned with Values

In a landscape where ethics can be murky, doubt allows us to **build relationships, partnerships, and commitments that are grounded in shared values**. By using doubt as a filter, we ensure that our connections are genuine, based on mutual respect and integrity. This approach to trust is particularly valuable in a world where surface appearances may be misleading, where promises may be empty, and where the motivations of others may not always align with our own.

For example, when forming a business partnership, doubt can guide us to seek out organizations that prioritize transparency, ethical practices, and social responsibility. This doesn't mean we mistrust all potential partners; instead, it means that we evaluate each option carefully to ensure that our values are reflected in the partnership. **Doubt helps us stay true to our principles**, ensuring that the relationships we invest in are ones that will genuinely contribute to our growth and align with our long-term vision.

Similarly, in personal relationships, doubt enables us to build connections that are both secure and aligned with our beliefs. When we approach relationships with a sense of discernment, we can identify people who not only respect our boundaries but also share our values. This creates a foundation for trust that is **rooted in authenticity and mutual respect**, allowing us to feel safe and supported. By allowing doubt to guide our choices, we create bonds that have the resilience to withstand challenges because they are based on a strong alignment of ideals and intentions.

Doubt as a Tool for Personal and Collective Growth

Incorporating doubt into our trust-building process isn't about closing ourselves off; it's about **creating a framework for growth**. When we trust thoughtfully, informed by doubt, we're more open to learning and evolving. We become aware of our boundaries, needs, and values, allowing us to engage with others in ways that support our growth rather than compromising our integrity. Doubt encourages us to reflect on our experiences, helping us to refine our understanding of who and what we can trust.

On a collective level, doubt fosters **cultures of accountability**. In workplaces, communities, and social circles, doubt encourages people to be transparent, to communicate openly, and to uphold ethical standards. It prevents the formation of echo chambers, where ideas go unchallenged and assumptions remain unquestioned. Instead, doubt invites people to engage in constructive dialogue, to verify claims, and to seek truth. This shared commitment to truth and accountability builds a culture of trust that is collective and resilient, one that's able to adapt to the changing ethical landscape.

In organizations, for instance, doubt can inspire the implementation of practices like regular audits, ethical training programs, and open communication policies. By embedding doubt into the organizational culture, companies can build **a strong foundation of integrity** that not only supports trust within the company but also strengthens its reputation in the eyes of clients, partners, and the public.

Trust Guided by Doubt: Empowerment Through Awareness

By incorporating doubt into our approach to trust, we shift from passive trust to **empowered, active trust**. We become co-creators of trust, making informed choices about whom and what we engage with. Doubt guides us to stay aware, to ask questions, and to seek clarity, creating a foundation for trust that is robust enough to handle the complexities of modern relationships and partnerships.

This approach also allows us to engage meaningfully with others without sacrificing our sense of security or autonomy. When we trust with discernment, we can feel confident in our connections, knowing that we've taken steps to protect ourselves while remaining open to new possibilities. **Trust guided by doubt enables us to navigate life with confidence and clarity**, grounded in the knowledge that our trust is not blind but well-informed, resilient, and aligned with our values.

Applying Doubt as a Constructive Tool in Everyday Life

As we continue, consider how doubt might serve as a constructive tool in your own life, whether in personal relationships, career decisions, or community engagements. Let doubt be a **guide that brings clarity and confidence**, helping you to build trust that is both deep and durable. Use doubt as a filter, evaluating actions, motives, and values to ensure that your trust is grounded in reality.

For example:

In relationships: Use doubt as a way to set healthy boundaries, taking time to observe others' actions before fully investing your trust. This approach allows trust to grow gradually, based on consistency and respect.

In professional settings: Allow doubt to prompt transparency and accountability, establishing clear expectations and performance standards. This fosters a culture where trust is earned through consistent actions rather than assumed.

In communities or organizations: Use doubt to engage thoughtfully, questioning claims, validating information, and supporting causes or groups that demonstrate ethical alignment. This ensures that your involvement is both meaningful and reflective of your principles.

The Enduring Strength of Trust Supported by Doubt

By embracing doubt as part of our trust-building process, we are creating a foundation for trust that has the **strength to endure**. This trust is not fragile or easily broken because it is grounded in reality, backed by discernment, and protected by boundaries. Trust supported by doubt is adaptable, able to withstand the pressures of a world that is often unpredictable and ethically ambiguous.

In an era where it can feel difficult to know whom or what to trust, doubt acts as our **silent guide**, ensuring that we are not led astray by idealism or assumption. It encourages us to cultivate relationships, partnerships, and commitments that are resilient, meaningful, and aligned with our values. Through doubt, we gain the freedom to engage fully, knowing that our trust is grounded in strength and clarity.

As we continue to explore the dynamics of trust and doubt, remember that these two forces are not at odds; they are complementary tools that empower us to navigate life with wisdom, resilience, and authenticity.

3: Building Trust with Boundaries—A Conditional Approach

Trust thrives when it is given with intention and supported by clear boundaries. In a world where motivations can be unpredictable and ethical lines blurred, unconditional trust is rarely practical. Instead, trust becomes a conditional, evolving process—one that is guided by mutually agreed-upon limits and responsibilities. Setting boundaries doesn't mean withholding trust; it means creating a space where trust can grow safely, supported by respect and accountability. This chapter explores how defining and communicating boundaries allows trust to flourish while protecting your well-being, enabling you to engage meaningfully without unnecessary risk.

Introducing Conditional Trust as a Practical Response to Unethical Settings

In a perfect world, trust might be absolute—a choice made with complete confidence in another person's intentions and integrity. However, in reality, where motivations can be mixed, pressures can influence behavior, and ethical standards may vary widely, **conditional trust offers a balanced and practical approach**. Conditional trust acknowledges the complexities and potential uncertainties of modern relationships and professional environments, where motivations aren't always transparent and ethical practices aren't always guaranteed. Rather than assuming trust as an all-or-nothing state, conditional trust allows us to establish **boundaries and expectations** that create a foundation of mutual accountability. This approach doesn't imply distrust; rather, it's a recognition that trust can be fragile and that it needs to be built on a foundation of understanding and consistent actions.

Conditional trust is an approach that allows us to engage meaningfully with others while protecting ourselves from potential disappointment, betrayal, or ethical compromise. It's a **practical response** to today's world, one that empowers us to trust without losing sight of self-protection and discernment. Conditional trust doesn't prevent us from connecting deeply with others; rather, it **strengthens relationships** by setting clear expectations, requiring consistency, and fostering accountability.

The Value of Boundaries and Gradual Trust-Building

By practicing conditional trust, we don't dive headfirst into relationships or commitments with blind faith. Instead, we place trust gradually, establishing **specific boundaries and conditions** that bring both clarity and security. These boundaries help us define the terms of engagement, allowing us to determine where our trust begins and where it might end if those terms aren't met. For instance, we might trust a new business partner to meet deadlines and provide honest feedback but set limits on sensitive information sharing until there's a demonstrated level of reliability.

Conditional trust offers a structured way to navigate relationships in ethically ambiguous environments, providing us with a reliable framework. Rather than exposing ourselves to the full range of risks that come with blind trust, we maintain a degree of control. Conditional trust is not rigid or punitive; rather, it's adaptable, allowing us to build trust step-by-step based on observable actions, demonstrated consistency, and alignment with shared values.

In settings where stakes are high—such as in business partnerships, legal matters, or personal relationships where we've previously experienced betrayal—conditional trust provides a **buffer of protection**. This approach allows us to navigate risks and ethical uncertainties without compromising our principles. It's a form of trust that is **anchored in reality**, supported by actions that align with our expectations rather than abstract promises.

Establishing Mutual Accountability through Conditional Trust

One of the essential elements of conditional trust is **mutual accountability**. By setting clear conditions, we establish a shared understanding of what each party is responsible for and what behaviors are expected. This reciprocity reinforces trust over time, as each party knows that trust is not something taken for granted but something earned through actions. Conditional trust empowers us to hold others accountable for their commitments, making it clear that trust is not a passive, unquestioned state but an **active, ongoing choice**.

For example, in a work environment where collaboration is necessary but motivations may not always be aligned, conditional trust helps create a framework of expectations. A team leader might trust their team members to complete their tasks on time, but also establish conditions that require regular check-ins, progress reports, or open communication about any challenges. By doing so, the leader fosters a workplace environment that values both trust and accountability, ensuring that **trust is built through transparency and follow-through**.

Conditional trust allows us to engage without feeling overly vulnerable because our trust is grounded in specific, observable actions. It ensures that we're not setting ourselves up for disappointment by expecting others to behave in ways they may not be prepared or able to meet. This **balanced approach to trust** allows us to create relationships that are both resilient and realistic, capable of adapting to challenges because they are grounded in a foundation of accountability.

The Strength of Conditional Trust in High-Stakes and Ethical Uncertainties

Conditional trust is particularly valuable in **high-stakes situations** where ethical standards may be ambiguous or where our values could be at risk. In these cases, trusting unconditionally could leave us vulnerable to unexpected outcomes or moral compromises. By setting conditions, we maintain a stance of **informed engagement**. This approach doesn't mean we're guarded or unwilling to collaborate; instead, it means that we are thoughtful, discerning, and intentional about whom we choose to trust and to what extent.

In high-stakes situations, conditional trust allows us to navigate **risks and ethical uncertainties without sacrificing our values**. It enables us to assess the trustworthiness of individuals and organizations based on concrete evidence rather than assumptions. For example, if entering a joint venture in an industry with varying ethical standards, one might trust a partner to meet financial goals but set conditions requiring ethical compliance audits and regular updates on their business practices. These conditions protect both parties, aligning actions with shared values and reducing the risk of moral compromise.

In personal relationships, conditional trust can also serve as a **pathway to healing** when trust has been broken in the past. If someone has experienced betrayal or disappointment, conditional trust allows them to re-enter relationships with a sense of security. They can set boundaries around vulnerable areas, allowing trust to grow gradually rather than feeling pressured to trust completely right away. This gradual approach not only protects the individual but also allows the relationship to rebuild on a foundation of **renewed respect and responsibility**.

Conditional Trust as a Tool for Empowerment and Connection

Through conditional trust, we gain the **freedom to connect with others while preserving our sense of autonomy and security**. This approach empowers us to trust deeply without feeling that we're risking our values, expectations, or emotional well-being. Conditional trust gives us the tools to engage meaningfully, creating connections based on mutual understanding and respect rather than blind reliance.

By setting boundaries and clear expectations, we avoid the emotional toll of having to repair trust after a disappointment or breach. Instead, we **protect our emotional and psychological well-being** from the outset by establishing the terms of trust from the very beginning. Conditional trust fosters a form of connection that feels secure, one that recognizes the potential for growth and change without sacrificing our needs and standards.

This framework is particularly helpful in maintaining balance between **openness and self-protection**. We're able to engage fully, open ourselves up to collaboration, and form relationships that are meaningful and lasting, without compromising our boundaries. Conditional trust allows us to explore new possibilities, whether in friendships, professional relationships, or partnerships, with a sense of clarity and confidence.

Setting Clear Boundaries to Define the Limits of Trust

Boundaries are essential to **defining the limits of trust**, allowing us to balance openness with self-protection. Trust, without boundaries, can lead to overextension, where we invest more than we should, potentially leaving ourselves vulnerable to disappointment or even betrayal. **Boundaries serve as a framework** that guides the extent and depth of our engagement in any relationship—personal, professional, or institutional. They help us clarify where our trust begins and where it ends, enabling us to trust without compromising our values or exposing ourselves unnecessarily to risk.

Boundaries help us to **trust selectively and sustainably**. Rather than shutting ourselves off from trust entirely or placing it indiscriminately, we can determine which areas are safe for engagement and which may require more caution. In a workplace setting, for example, you might trust a colleague to collaborate on projects and share work-related ideas, but you might choose to keep personal information private until there's sufficient evidence of reliability. Similarly, in personal relationships, boundaries allow us to **pace trust**, letting it grow gradually as consistency and reliability are demonstrated over time.

How Boundaries Protect Emotional and Psychological Well-being

Setting boundaries helps us maintain **emotional and psychological well-being** by ensuring that trust is given mindfully and responsibly. Without boundaries, we might find ourselves repeatedly overcommitted or emotionally invested in relationships or situations that drain us. Boundaries prevent this by establishing **limits on our availability, energy, and expectations**. They act as a form of self-care, allowing us to stay connected without feeling overwhelmed or vulnerable to those who may not have our best interests at heart.

Boundaries give us permission to say "no" or to step back when a situation feels uncomfortable or misaligned with our values. For instance, in a new friendship, setting a boundary around emotional openness might mean choosing to share general information but waiting until you're sure of the person's trustworthiness before discussing deeper, personal topics. This **step-by-step approach** to building trust keeps us emotionally grounded, as it allows time for a relationship to prove its stability and reliability before we invest more of ourselves.

In professional environments, boundaries prevent us from overcommitting to tasks that might jeopardize our well-being or interfere with our other responsibilities. For example, you may trust your team to manage a shared project, but you might set boundaries around your availability for non-urgent requests. This helps you maintain **a balanced workflow**, enabling you to contribute effectively without experiencing burnout. By establishing these boundaries early on, you create a sustainable approach to trust, one that preserves your mental and emotional energy.

Defining Specific Areas for Trust and Caution

Boundaries don't mean shutting off trust entirely; they mean **differentiating between areas where trust can be extended confidently and areas where caution is advisable**. Setting these boundaries can take many forms, depending on the context and the individuals involved. Here's how boundaries can be applied in different situations:

Workplace Relationships: In professional settings, trust may be necessary for effective collaboration, but boundaries can define where that trust extends. You might trust a colleague to provide honest feedback on a project but decide to keep personal information private until you're confident in their discretion. Similarly, you may set boundaries around your working hours to prevent an imbalance between professional and personal life.

Personal Relationships: In friendships or romantic relationships, trust often grows in layers. You might begin by sharing general information and then slowly expand to more personal topics as reliability is demonstrated. Boundaries here allow you to pace the relationship, ensuring that trust is built gradually rather than all at once.

Institutional Trust: When dealing with organizations, such as banks, schools, or healthcare providers, boundaries might involve assessing which aspects of the institution can be trusted and where you need to take additional precautions. For example, while you might trust a hospital with your general care, you might set boundaries by asking questions, seeking second opinions, or reviewing policies on patient privacy to ensure your needs and safety are prioritized.

These boundaries help us **differentiate between areas of trust and areas of caution**, enabling us to engage in relationships without feeling overexposed or uncertain. By setting limits, we take control of how much trust we extend, safeguarding ourselves from potential disappointments or breaches.

Creating Sustainable and Adaptable Trust through Boundaries

Boundaries ensure that trust remains **sustainable and adaptable**. When we trust without boundaries, we risk becoming overly invested, making it difficult to adjust if things don't go as expected. With boundaries, however, we can allow trust to evolve naturally, adapting our expectations as new information or experiences emerge. This approach empowers us to remain open and engaged in our relationships and commitments while protecting ourselves from overextension or potential harm.

Boundaries also allow us to **respond to changes** in relationships. If a friend who was once reliable becomes inconsistent, the boundary of trust can be adjusted to reflect this change, helping us to protect our emotional investment. Similarly, in a work environment, if a trusted colleague begins missing deadlines or delivering incomplete work, boundaries can shift to limit reliance on their contributions until consistency is restored. This adaptability is key to **maintaining a balanced approach to trust**, ensuring that our relationships and commitments remain supportive rather than draining.

Boundaries make trust dynamic and resilient, ready to evolve with circumstances while protecting our emotional and psychological health. This approach is particularly valuable in long-term relationships, where boundaries can shift and adapt over time, reflecting the natural ebb and flow of shared experiences.

Guiding Others through Clear Boundaries

Boundaries serve as a **guide for others**, helping them understand what is expected and respected in the relationship. When we set boundaries and communicate them openly, we clarify the **terms of engagement** for trust. This doesn't mean imposing rigid limits; rather, it's about creating a framework where trust can grow while honoring each person's needs and values.

For instance, in a professional setting, communicating boundaries about availability helps colleagues know when they can expect a response and when they need to wait. This encourages respect for each other's time and reduces the likelihood of misunderstandings or unmet expectations. In personal relationships, expressing boundaries around communication or time spent together helps friends or partners understand what makes you feel secure and respected, creating an environment of **mutual understanding**.

Clear boundaries not only protect us but also offer others the opportunity to demonstrate their reliability and respect for our needs. This creates a relationship dynamic in which both parties feel secure, appreciated, and valued. Boundaries don't limit the potential for connection; they create the conditions for **healthy, sustainable trust** that can withstand the challenges of everyday life.

Crafting Boundaries Reflective of Our Values, Needs, and Experiences

By setting clear limits, we create a version of trust that is **resilient and reflective of our needs, values, and experiences**. Our boundaries should be unique to us, grounded in our beliefs, past experiences, and personal standards. Rather than conforming to a "one-size-fits-all" approach to trust, boundaries allow us to define trust in ways that feel right for us and that honor our individual perspectives.

For example, someone who values privacy highly may set more cautious boundaries in sharing personal information, trusting others only as they prove themselves reliable. Someone else, who values open communication, might set boundaries around honesty and transparency, ensuring that trust is grounded in shared authenticity. Our boundaries reflect our **priorities, our values, and our comfort zones**, enabling us to engage in relationships and commitments in ways that feel authentic and aligned with who we are.

Boundaries also provide the flexibility to adapt over time as we gain new experiences and insights. As we become more confident in our relationships, we might adjust boundaries to allow for deeper trust. Conversely, if trust is broken, boundaries give us a clear way to step back, protecting ourselves without feeling guilty or resentful. This adaptability allows us to **navigate trust with confidence**, knowing that we can honor our needs without feeling trapped by obligations.

Boundaries as a Tool for Empowering Connection and Self-Care

Setting boundaries isn't about isolating ourselves; it's a tool for empowering connection and practicing self-care. When we establish boundaries, we engage with others **from a place of strength and security**, knowing that our limits are respected. This creates a foundation for meaningful interactions, allowing us to connect deeply without sacrificing our emotional health. Boundaries let us enjoy relationships in a way that feels enriching and balanced, making space for connection without compromising self-respect.

In an era where expectations and obligations can be overwhelming, boundaries remind us that we are allowed to protect our time, energy, and values. They enable us to **say "yes" to trust in a way that is safe and intentional**. Boundaries give us the freedom to connect meaningfully, with the assurance that we are in control of how much we give and what we allow.

As we continue to explore the role of trust and boundaries, consider how these principles might apply in your own relationships. Setting boundaries doesn't restrict your potential for trust; rather, it lays the groundwork for trust to grow responsibly. With clear limits, trust becomes a source of connection and fulfillment, reflective of your values and supportive of your well-being.

Guidance on Establishing and Communicating Conditions in Trust

Conditional trust requires establishing and **clearly communicating conditions** that define the relationship's boundaries and expectations. This approach doesn't signify a lack of trust; rather, it enhances the quality and reliability of trust by ensuring that both parties understand what is expected of them and are held accountable. In settings where stakes are high—whether in business, personal relationships, or situations involving significant risks—these conditions serve as a foundation for a relationship based on mutual respect and reliability. Here's how to apply conditional trust across various areas of life:

In Business Settings

In business, conditional trust is crucial, especially when collaborating with new partners, clients, or suppliers. The competitive nature of business often means motivations can differ, and trust should not be assumed without verification. By setting conditions, we create a **framework for accountability and transparency** that supports a sustainable business relationship.

Define Expectations and Responsibilities: In any business relationship, clarity around roles and responsibilities is essential. Take the time to **define deliverables, deadlines, and scope of work**, and put these agreements in writing. This step reduces miscommunication and provides a reference point to ensure that both parties understand and meet their obligations. For example, a partnership agreement might specify the exact deliverables each partner is responsible for and the timeline for completion.

Set Up Regular Checkpoints: Periodic evaluations provide an opportunity for both parties to review progress, address challenges, and make adjustments as needed. **Checkpoints reinforce accountability**, allowing trust to build gradually based on demonstrated reliability and a commitment to shared goals. For instance, scheduling monthly progress meetings to assess the status of a project can help ensure that both parties are on track and aligned.

Communicate Consequences and Adjustments: Be clear that the terms of the partnership will evolve based on performance. If certain conditions are not met, outline the steps that will be taken to address these issues, which might involve **renegotiation, additional oversight, or adjustments** to the scope of trust. For example, if a supplier repeatedly fails to meet deadlines, the business may reduce order quantities or renegotiate delivery timelines.

These boundaries establish a foundation for business partnerships that are **resilient to challenges** and grounded in measurable actions and mutual accountability. Both parties benefit from a relationship that is fair, transparent, and adaptable to evolving needs, ultimately enhancing productivity and cooperation.

In Personal Relationships

In personal relationships, conditional trust is key to building meaningful connections while protecting emotional well-being. Conditional trust allows us to engage authentically, pacing trust based on observed behavior, reliability, and consistency. This approach does not involve constant doubt but rather **creating a balance between openness and self-respect**.

Pace Trust Gradually: Allow trust to grow with the relationship, observing how the other person handles shared confidences, responsibilities, and support. If they demonstrate reliability and understanding over time, **trust can deepen naturally**. For example, you might begin by sharing general life details with a new friend, gradually opening up as they show they can be supportive and trustworthy.

Set Emotional Boundaries: Determine which areas of your life are open for sharing and which are protected until there is a demonstrated level of trustworthiness. For example, while you might discuss work or hobbies early on in a friendship, you might wait to share more intimate concerns until a deeper trust has been established. These boundaries help prevent emotional overexposure and ensure that trust is built at a comfortable, steady pace.

Communicate Needs and Expectations: Explain to the other person what trust looks like for you and share your expectations. Discussing boundaries around personal space, honesty, or time commitments can create a **mutual understanding** of how to navigate the relationship. For example, if honesty is a priority, you might express that trust grows best when each person feels free to be authentic and open about their feelings.

By applying these practices, we create a sustainable foundation for trust that fosters deep, resilient connections without compromising emotional safety. Conditional trust allows us to engage wholeheartedly, knowing that boundaries are in place to protect well-being and respect individual comfort levels.

In High-Stakes Scenarios

In high-stakes scenarios, such as healthcare, legal matters, or financial investments, conditional trust becomes even more critical. Here, the potential consequences of misplaced trust are substantial, so it's essential to **approach**

these relationships with discernment and clear conditions. This structured approach to trust ensures that decisions are based on thorough evaluation and reliable evidence.

Verify Credentials and Track Records: Before committing to high-stakes decisions, research the credentials and past performance of the people or institutions involved. This step helps confirm that they meet necessary standards and have a reliable history. For instance, in healthcare, you might verify a surgeon's qualifications and reviews before agreeing to a procedure. In investments, researching a financial advisor's track record and certifications can help establish a foundation of informed trust.

Set Clear Accountability Measures: Establish specific accountability measures, such as contracts, progress reports, or third-party audits, depending on the situation. This ensures that **all parties adhere to agreed-upon standards** and provides a way to monitor actions and outcomes. For example, in real estate transactions, involving an independent inspector to verify property condition safeguards trust and ensures all parties are aligned with transparency.

Outline Contingency Plans: In high-stakes settings, planning for setbacks can make a significant difference. **Create contingency plans** that outline steps to take if certain conditions are not met, such as transferring responsibilities, revising contracts, or bringing in additional resources. For instance, in a business partnership, you might establish an exit strategy or an agreement for mediation if conflicts arise.

Conditional trust in these scenarios allows us to engage meaningfully while **minimizing risk**. By setting clear expectations, verifying reliability, and planning for contingencies, we create an environment where trust can be confidently extended without the fear of unchecked vulnerability.

Benefits of Establishing and Communicating Conditions in Trust

Establishing and communicating conditions in trust offers multiple benefits across different areas of life, including:

Clarity and Alignment: Conditions clarify what each party can expect and what is required, ensuring everyone is aligned with the same goals and standards.

Reduced Misunderstandings: When expectations are explicitly stated, there is less room for misinterpretation, which reduces conflicts and confusion.

Adaptability: Conditional trust allows relationships to adjust and evolve based on performance, actions, and changing needs, making them more resilient to unexpected challenges.

Empowerment Through Accountability: Conditions empower both parties to uphold their responsibilities, fostering a sense of accountability and pride in fulfilling commitments.

Practical Steps for Communicating Conditions Effectively

To establish and communicate conditions in trust effectively, consider the following steps:

Be Transparent and Direct: When setting conditions, be open and honest. Share the reasons behind your conditions, expressing how they will support a healthy relationship or partnership. For example, "I'd like to start with weekly check-ins so we can stay on the same page as we move forward."

Listen to the Other Party's Perspective: Establishing trust is a two-way process, and it's crucial to listen to the other person's needs and expectations. Understanding their perspective can help in **adjusting conditions** to create a balanced foundation for trust.

Focus on Mutual Benefit: Emphasize that conditions benefit both parties by making the relationship or partnership more reliable and transparent. Communicate that conditions are not about control or doubt, but rather about fostering a dynamic that supports **fairness and accountability**.

Use Positive, Constructive Language: When communicating conditions, frame them in a way that feels empowering rather than restrictive. For example, instead of saying, "I don't want you to share my personal information," try, "I trust that you'll keep what we discuss here confidential."

Reinforce Boundaries Through Actions: Follow through on the conditions you've established. For instance, if you've set a boundary about regular updates, make sure to request or provide those updates consistently.

Reinforcing conditions through actions demonstrates that the boundaries you've set are important.

Revisit and Adjust as Needed: Conditions in trust don't have to be static. As relationships and situations evolve, periodically assess whether adjustments are necessary. This flexibility keeps trust adaptable, ensuring it remains aligned with current circumstances.

Creating a Trust Framework for the Long Term

By setting and communicating conditions, we're able to create a **trust framework that's sustainable for the long term**. Conditional trust provides a pathway for relationships to grow authentically, balancing openness with discernment and accountability. When trust is conditional, it becomes a dynamic and flexible process, one that reflects our values and provides a sturdy foundation for connection in complex environments.

Conditions provide clarity, reduce misunderstandings, and empower relationships to evolve based on reliability and shared expectations. Trust becomes a **shared commitment to mutual benefit**, where both parties feel valued and accountable. Whether in business, personal life, or high-stakes scenarios, conditional trust helps us engage responsibly, ensuring that trust is a source of strength, resilience, and integrity.

Balancing Openness with Self-Protection

Conditional trust is a tool for balancing **openness with self-protection**, allowing us to engage meaningfully in relationships without compromising our security or well-being. In a world where motivations are diverse and trustworthiness can vary, this balance is essential for maintaining healthy, resilient relationships. By defining the terms of trust and establishing clear boundaries, we are able to connect with others in a way that is both grounded and protective. This approach ensures that our trust is given thoughtfully and intentionally, without leaving us overly vulnerable to the unpredictability of others' actions or motives.

Openness: Trust with Awareness and Boundaries

Conditional trust doesn't mean that we close ourselves off or adopt a guarded stance in our relationships. Rather, it's about **remaining open while setting parameters** that make engagement safe and fulfilling. With conditional trust, we can extend trust without naivety, staying open to connection while ensuring that our expectations are realistic and based on observable actions and shared values.

Openness in conditional trust involves:

Assessing and Observing Actions: Openness under conditional trust means that we allow others to demonstrate their trustworthiness over time. We don't assume that trust is automatic; instead, we watch for consistency in actions that align with our values. This approach allows us to remain receptive without feeling pressured to trust prematurely.

Creating Space for Connection: Conditional trust is about creating a space where trust can grow authentically. By setting boundaries and conditions, we give ourselves permission to connect without hesitation, knowing that we've established limits that protect us. For example, in a new friendship, we might choose to be open to spending time together while waiting to share personal details until trust is proven through consistency and mutual respect.

Supporting Authenticity in Relationships: When we establish conditional trust, we also encourage others to be genuine, as they understand that trust will be extended based on observable, reliable behavior. This creates a foundation of authenticity, as both parties feel comfortable being themselves, knowing that trust is realistic rather than idealistic.

This form of trust fosters **honest, real connections**, where openness is balanced with practical awareness. Conditional trust empowers us to engage fully and meaningfully while ensuring that our trust remains rooted in reality.

Self-Protection: Creating a Safety Net with Boundaries and Conditions

Boundaries and conditions create a **safety net** in conditional trust, helping us avoid overexposure or misplaced trust. This protective layer doesn't imply a lack of confidence in others; rather, it allows us to safeguard our well-being and invest in relationships thoughtfully. By setting boundaries, we establish clear guidelines on where trust can be extended and where it may need to be limited.

Self-protection in conditional trust includes:

Setting Boundaries that Reflect Personal Values: Boundaries help us align our trust with our values and priorities, guiding us on how much we are willing to share or depend on others. For example, in a professional setting, we may establish boundaries around availability, ensuring that work-life balance is maintained. This enables us to engage productively without risking burnout or overextension.

Limiting Overexposure in Vulnerable Areas: Conditional trust allows us to protect sensitive aspects of our lives by controlling when, how, and to whom we reveal them. In personal relationships, for instance, we might reserve certain emotional disclosures until the other person has demonstrated their reliability. This gradual approach minimizes the risk of feeling exposed or betrayed if the relationship doesn't evolve as hoped.

Recovering Quickly from Breaches of Trust: If trust is broken, the boundaries we've set allow us to recover more easily, as we've defined limits that prevent deep emotional harm. When trust is given conditionally, we're less likely to feel devastated by a breach, as we haven't invested in the relationship unreservedly. This protective layer fosters resilience, enabling us to adjust our engagement without experiencing undue vulnerability.

Self-protection through boundaries **ensures that trust is manageable**, helping us avoid emotional overinvestment or dependency on others. By recognizing that trust can be both extended and withheld based on actions, we gain confidence in our ability to protect ourselves while remaining open to meaningful connections.

Finding Balance for Confident and Authentic Trust

This balance between openness and self-protection allows us to trust with confidence, knowing that **our boundaries keep us grounded**. Conditional trust gives us the freedom to engage with others while maintaining a clear sense of our needs, values, and expectations. Instead of being either overly trusting or excessively guarded, we can find a middle ground that feels safe yet enriching.

Balancing openness with self-protection also supports:

Empowered Decision-Making: With conditional trust, we choose to whom we give trust and in what circumstances. This sense of agency ensures that we are not just passively extending trust but actively participating in building relationships that align with our standards.

Resilient Relationships: Trust built with this balance is often more resilient, as it grows from a foundation of clear boundaries and mutual respect. We're able to adjust our trust as the relationship evolves, supporting connections that can withstand challenges and adapt to change.

Reduced Emotional Strain: By setting clear terms for trust, we avoid the emotional toll that can come from misplaced or unregulated trust. Knowing that we have protective measures in place, we can engage without fear, reducing stress and allowing for healthier, more stable relationships.

Ultimately, conditional trust empowers us to navigate relationships with **clarity and confidence**. We can open up to others in ways that are safe and sustainable, trusting with a balance that honors both our need for connection and our right to self-protection.

Communicating Conditions for Trust: Practical Steps

Establishing conditional trust involves not only setting boundaries but also **communicating them clearly** to others. Effective communication of these boundaries is essential for building trust that is respectful, accountable, and sustainable. It ensures that both parties understand the expectations, creating a foundation for a relationship where trust can grow over time. Here are practical steps for effectively expressing the conditions of your trust:

Clarify Your Boundaries First

Before communicating conditions to others, **take time to identify and clarify your boundaries**. Ask yourself what is essential for you to feel secure and respected in the relationship or engagement. This self-reflection helps you define what you need for trust to flourish and ensures you're confident in expressing these boundaries.

Identify Priorities and Deal-Breakers: Determine which conditions are non-negotiable for you. For example, in a professional relationship, reliability and transparency might be essential, while in personal relationships, emotional honesty and consistency may take precedence.

Understand the Purpose of Each Boundary: Recognize why each boundary is important to you. If privacy is essential, for instance, be clear about the areas where you want to maintain privacy and the reasons behind it. Knowing the "why" behind each boundary makes it easier to convey it confidently.

By clarifying your boundaries first, you're better prepared to **articulate them effectively** and ensure they align with your values and needs.

Use Direct and Respectful Language

When discussing conditions, **communicate with both clarity and respect**. Being direct ensures that your boundaries are understood, while respectful language fosters a constructive conversation. Rather than framing conditions as restrictive, present them as supportive measures that help build trust.

Express Boundaries as Enablers of Openness: Instead of saying, "I don't want you to do X," try framing it as, "Having clear boundaries around X allows me to feel more comfortable and open in our relationship."

Avoid Blame or Assumptions: Focus on your needs rather than implying that the other person is untrustworthy. For example, say, "I prefer regular communication to feel connected," rather than, "I don't trust people who don't communicate often."

Direct and respectful language ensures that your boundaries are communicated **positively and effectively**. This approach opens a pathway for understanding rather than creating tension or defensiveness.

Focus on Mutual Benefit

Emphasize that boundaries benefit **both parties** by creating a relationship based on clear expectations and mutual respect. When boundaries are communicated as mutual supports rather than restrictions, the other person is more likely to appreciate their value.

Explain the Purpose of Boundaries for the Relationship: For example, in a work context, you might say, "Regular check-ins help both of us stay aligned and address issues early on, making the project more successful."

Highlight Boundaries as a Pathway to Trust: Let the other person know that these conditions are designed to build a relationship where trust is reliable and secure. For example, "I feel more at ease sharing personal things when I know that our conversations are kept private."

Focusing on mutual benefits reframes conditions as **positive contributions** to the relationship, helping both parties feel valued and respected.

Be Consistent with Follow-Through

Once boundaries are established, it's crucial to **be consistent with follow-through**. This reinforces that your boundaries are important and signals that they are not flexible under pressure. Consistency establishes trust in your word and actions, showing others that you are serious about maintaining respectful limits.

Maintain Boundaries Even in Difficult Situations: If a friend or colleague tries to push past a set boundary, calmly remind them of the agreed-upon limits. This reinforces the importance of your conditions and helps avoid exceptions that might undermine trust.

Model the Boundaries for Others: By adhering to your own boundaries, you set an example. For instance, if you've requested punctuality in meetings, ensure that you also arrive on time. This demonstrates that boundaries are mutual and respected on both sides.

Consistency with follow-through **solidifies trust** by showing that your boundaries are non-negotiable and serve as a stable framework for the relationship.

Reassess and Adjust as Needed

As relationships evolve, periodically **review and adjust your boundaries**. Trust may deepen, and as mutual respect grows, some boundaries can be relaxed or redefined. Similarly, if issues arise, certain boundaries might need to be reinforced or adjusted.

Assess Boundaries in the Context of Relationship Growth: In a personal relationship, as trust strengthens, you might choose to share more sensitive information or relax certain limitations. For instance, if a friend consistently respects your need for privacy, you may gradually feel comfortable sharing more.

Stay Open to Feedback: Encourage the other person to share their thoughts on the boundaries. If they feel a certain condition limits the relationship, discuss possible adjustments that feel comfortable for both parties.

Adapt Boundaries to Changing Situations: Life circumstances may change, affecting the relevance of certain boundaries. Be flexible and open to reassessing them in a way that respects both your needs and those of the other party.

Regularly reassessing and adjusting boundaries ensures that trust remains **relevant, responsive, and supportive** as relationships develop over time.

Building a Foundation of Understanding and Respect

These steps create a foundation for **open, respectful communication** that allows conditional trust to thrive. By sharing your conditions clearly and engaging others in a conversation about boundaries, you set the stage for relationships that are grounded in understanding, accountability, and mutual respect.

Communicating conditions for trust enables relationships to grow with **both security and freedom**, allowing each person to feel respected and valued. This approach helps to avoid misunderstandings, build trust gradually, and foster deeper connections, creating a trust framework that's resilient, flexible, and empowering for everyone involved.

The Power of Conditional Trust

In a world where motivations can be complex and trust cannot always be assumed, **conditional trust provides a powerful framework** for navigating relationships responsibly. By setting boundaries and establishing conditions, we create a form of trust that is adaptable, resilient, and grounded in our core values. Conditional trust doesn't require us to abandon our openness; rather, it enables us to extend trust thoughtfully and responsibly, engaging in relationships that reflect our principles while respecting the complexities of human interactions.

Conditional trust encourages us to **evaluate trust on an individual basis** rather than adopting a "one-size-fits-all" approach. It acknowledges that different situations, personalities, and relationships require different levels of openness and caution. By embracing this nuanced perspective, we empower ourselves to connect with others authentically while protecting our well-being. In an uncertain world, conditional trust provides the tools to **engage without feeling vulnerable**. We can remain open to forming connections without sacrificing self-respect or exposing ourselves to unwarranted risks.

Trust That Reflects Our Values

Conditional trust gives us the freedom to **build relationships that align with our values**. Instead of feeling pressured to trust indiscriminately, we can choose where to place our trust based on consistent actions, shared ethics, and demonstrated integrity. This approach allows us to create connections that feel genuine and fulfilling, as they are rooted in mutual respect and accountability.

For instance, in a work setting, conditional trust might mean setting clear expectations about communication and responsibility with colleagues or business partners. You trust them to uphold professional standards, but this trust is balanced with boundaries that ensure ethical practices. Similarly, in personal relationships, conditional trust means engaging fully with friends or loved ones while pacing your emotional investment based on consistency and support. These relationships grow in depth over time as trust is continually reinforced by reliable behavior.

In this way, conditional trust becomes a **method of cultivating connections that honor our principles**, creating relationships that bring fulfillment without compromising our sense of self.

Resilience and Adaptability in Trust

The strength of conditional trust lies in its **resilience and adaptability**. Rather than placing blind faith in others, we allow trust to evolve gradually, adjusting our boundaries and expectations based on actions and circumstances.

Conditional trust is not rigid; it's flexible, able to expand or contract in response to changing dynamics.

Resilience in the Face of Setbacks: Conditional trust acts as a safeguard, helping us to withstand disappointments and setbacks without becoming disillusioned. If someone fails to meet our expectations, we are less likely to feel blindsided because our trust was given with caution and boundaries. This resilience enables us to recover quickly and make informed decisions about future engagement.

Adaptability in Diverse Situations: Conditional trust allows us to adapt our trust levels based on individual relationships. In high-stakes situations, such as healthcare or legal matters, we can set strict conditions to protect our interests. In lower-stakes or more informal relationships, we might establish more lenient conditions, allowing trust to grow naturally over time.

This resilience and adaptability enable us to approach relationships with confidence and **without fear of betrayal**. Conditional trust offers a middle ground between blind faith and guarded cynicism, creating a version of trust that is both realistic and durable.

Empowerment Through Accountability and Mutual Respect

Conditional trust fosters **mutual respect and accountability**, transforming relationships into partnerships where both parties contribute actively to maintaining trust. This approach empowers us to engage fully, knowing that both sides are held accountable for their actions. It's a model of trust that encourages honest communication and reinforces boundaries as a means of building deeper, more enduring connections.

Encouraging Mutual Accountability: When conditions are clearly defined, both parties understand that trust is earned and sustained through consistent behavior. This fosters an environment where each person feels responsible for upholding the standards of the relationship. For example, in a collaborative work project, conditional trust might involve regular check-ins and accountability measures that ensure everyone is fulfilling their commitments.

Creating Respectful Relationships: Conditional trust also reinforces respect, as it gives both parties the opportunity to demonstrate reliability over time. This model of trust removes the pressure of proving oneself immediately, allowing trust to grow organically through actions and shared experiences.

By incorporating conditional trust, we cultivate relationships where **honesty, respect, and accountability** form the foundation. This type of engagement allows for more profound connections, as both sides are aligned in their dedication to maintaining trust.

Freedom to Engage Meaningfully While Protecting Well-being

One of the most empowering aspects of conditional trust is that it allows us to **engage meaningfully without compromising our security**. We can connect deeply with others while feeling confident that our boundaries will protect us from overexposure or emotional harm. Conditional trust encourages us to interact with an open heart while maintaining clarity about our limits.

This balance between openness and self-protection is vital in a world where trustworthiness may be uncertain. Conditional trust lets us explore new connections, take calculated risks, and invest in relationships that have the potential to grow into something meaningful. We are free to be open and present without feeling pressured to abandon our needs or safety.

Using Conditional Trust as a Guide in Everyday Life

As we continue to navigate complex social, personal, and professional landscapes, conditional trust serves as a practical guide, helping us make **decisions rooted in clarity and self-respect**. By treating trust as a process rather than a fixed state, we create relationships that are fulfilling, genuine, and capable of withstanding the inevitable complexities of life.

In Personal Life: In friendships and family relationships, conditional trust allows us to pace emotional investment, gradually deepening connections as reliability is demonstrated. This approach helps prevent emotional burnout and supports a balanced, healthy approach to intimacy.

In Professional Life: Conditional trust in professional settings promotes accountability, collaboration, and productivity. By setting clear conditions, we create a work environment where everyone understands expectations and is motivated to uphold them.

In Community Engagements: In social or community-based relationships, conditional trust allows us to contribute meaningfully while setting boundaries that honor our values. It encourages us to engage with causes or groups that align with our principles, supporting respectful and impactful collaboration.

Embracing Conditional Trust for Clarity and Self-Respect

Embracing conditional trust is a **commitment to clarity and self-respect**. This approach empowers us to take control of our relationships, engage from a place of strength, and avoid the pitfalls of blind trust or cynicism. By practicing conditional trust, we create a framework that respects our boundaries, aligns with our values, and enables us to navigate uncertainty with confidence.

In a world where trust can be complex and multifaceted, conditional trust is a choice—a conscious decision to engage meaningfully while honoring our personal boundaries. This approach enriches our connections, ensuring that each relationship is a reflection of mutual respect, accountability, and shared purpose. By embracing conditional trust, we cultivate relationships, partnerships, and connections that can **flourish even in a world of uncertainty**.

4: The Role of Verification—Trust Through Accountability

Verification plays a critical role in **building and sustaining trust**. While trust often begins with a leap of faith or an initial sense of confidence, verification ensures that it is maintained and strengthened over time. Verification isn't about undermining trust; it's about reinforcing it through measurable actions. By incorporating accountability into trust, we create a solid foundation that withstands the complexities of relationships, allowing trust to grow stronger without leaving us vulnerable to disappointment or betrayal.

Doubt serves as the **catalyst for verification**. Rather than allowing doubt to erode trust, we use it to initiate actions that confirm and validate the reliability of others. Verification turns doubt into a constructive tool, empowering us to trust thoughtfully, informed by evidence and observation. This approach leads to **trust that is based on real actions and accountability** rather than assumptions.

How Verification Reinforces Trust Through Accountability

Verification serves as a powerful mechanism that transforms **assumptions into confirmations**. By incorporating regular checks and accountability, verification allows us to see firsthand that trust is based on actions that align with expectations. This approach doesn't mean we are constantly questioning others' intentions; rather, it's about ensuring that trust is sustained through observable, consistent actions. In personal, professional, and organizational relationships, verification allows us to measure **reliability, transparency, and commitment**—key elements that keep trust strong and resilient.

Building Confidence Through Consistency

Verification builds confidence in relationships by creating a **track record of reliability**. Every time we verify that a commitment has been met or a responsibility fulfilled, our trust in the other person grows. This process establishes a pattern of dependability that reinforces our sense of security and confidence in the relationship.

Establishing a History of Trustworthiness: Regular verification helps establish a history of trustworthy behavior. When we see that someone consistently meets their commitments—whether it's a friend showing up when they say they will, or a colleague delivering work on time—we begin to rely on that pattern. In work settings, for instance, verifying that project deadlines are met consistently builds a foundation of trust, reassuring us that we can depend on our team members.

Increasing Trust with Incremental Proof: Every successful verification is a small confirmation that builds up over time, gradually deepening trust. We no longer rely on hope or assumption but on **observable evidence** that the other party is reliable. This pattern of accountability allows us to extend trust more fully as we witness consistency, reducing any lingering doubts and replacing them with tangible proof.

This process of building confidence through consistent follow-through is essential in any relationship where reliability and predictability are valued. Verification in this way transforms trust into a **solid, reliable foundation** that withstands challenges and change.

Encouraging Transparency and Open Communication

Verification encourages **open and honest communication** by creating opportunities for both parties to discuss expectations, clarify any misunderstandings, and ensure alignment. This fosters an environment where both sides feel comfortable sharing their needs and concerns, reinforcing trust through transparency.

Creating a Platform for Addressing Discrepancies: Verification provides a natural opportunity to address discrepancies without causing conflict. When actions or outcomes don't align with expectations, a discussion can clarify the issue and provide solutions. For example, if a project's timeline is delayed, regular check-ins allow team members to discuss and adjust without misinterpretations building up. These conversations maintain the relationship's integrity by reinforcing trust through open, constructive feedback.

Normalizing Accountability as a Trust Practice: By integrating verification as a routine part of the relationship, accountability becomes a normalized practice rather than something unusual or punitive. Both parties understand that trust isn't assumed unconditionally but actively maintained. This approach encourages honesty, as everyone is aware that their actions will be reviewed in a supportive, nonjudgmental environment.

Promoting Mutual Respect and Ownership: When both parties are aware of expectations and the accountability measures in place, they are more likely to take ownership of their responsibilities. Verification reinforces a sense of mutual respect, as it shows that both sides value the integrity and consistency of the relationship enough to uphold accountability. This shared ownership of trust strengthens the bond between individuals, organizations, or teams.

Encouraging transparency through verification creates a space where **trust is both protected and reinforced**. Rather than leaving trust up to chance, this method ensures that trust is continually nurtured through open, respectful communication and aligned actions.

Trust That Is Grounded in Reality, Not Assumptions

When we integrate verification as a part of our trust-building process, we create **relationships grounded in reality**. Verification ensures that trust is based on actual behavior rather than assumptions, giving both parties a realistic view of each other's reliability and commitment. This approach leads to a form of trust that is resilient and adaptive, able to grow stronger over time without the risk of blind faith or unrealistic expectations.

Minimizing Risk of Disappointment: By verifying actions and commitments, we reduce the risk of being let down by unmet expectations. Verification allows us to adjust our level of trust according to observed actions, creating a more realistic and balanced perspective of the relationship. This approach fosters a kind of trust that is less likely to be shattered by isolated incidents because it is based on a pattern of consistent behavior rather than on idealized assumptions.

Strengthening Trust with Evidence-Based Confidence: Trust that is verified and reinforced through accountability is naturally more robust, as it's built on evidence rather than wishful thinking. Verification reassures us that our trust is well-placed, allowing us to rely on others with confidence. This solid foundation of trust is less likely to waiver under pressure because it has been tested and proven over time.

In relationships where verification is a regular practice, trust is **rooted in measurable reliability and consistent transparency**. This creates a bond that's stronger, more resilient, and capable of enduring challenges and changes over time.

Creating Resilient Relationships Through Accountability

By reinforcing trust through accountability, we foster relationships that are both resilient and flexible. Verification doesn't diminish trust; instead, it empowers us to navigate relationships with clarity, ensuring that trust is continually supported by evidence and aligned actions.

Verification also has a positive impact on the relationship itself, making it:

Less Susceptible to Misunderstandings: When expectations are discussed and verified regularly, misunderstandings are less likely to arise. The relationship becomes a partnership where each person's actions reinforce shared goals, making it easier to address potential issues before they escalate.

More Adaptive to Change: Relationships built on verified trust are better equipped to handle change, as both parties are accustomed to adapting based on consistent feedback. This adaptability allows the relationship to evolve, maintaining trust even as circumstances shift.

Ultimately, verification through accountability fosters **relationships that are durable and based on mutual respect**. By transforming trust from a passive assumption into an active, evidence-based practice, verification creates a type of trust that can withstand the complexities of real-life interactions. In doing so, it allows us to form connections that are not only reliable but also deeply satisfying, grounded in the security of consistency and the strength of transparency.

Methods for Maintaining Accountability Without

Compromising Integrity

Introducing verification practices doesn't mean approaching relationships with a skeptical or distrustful mindset. **Maintaining accountability** can be achieved in ways that support and strengthen trust while respecting the relationship's integrity. When approached thoughtfully, verification can reinforce mutual respect, open communication, and shared goals. Here are methods to establish accountability while preserving integrity:

Regular Check-Ins and Updates

Scheduling regular check-ins offers a structured opportunity to **review commitments, share progress, and address challenges**. These check-ins are not about scrutinizing each other but about creating a consistent space for collaboration and alignment.

Setting a Routine for Progress Reviews: In professional relationships, these could be weekly or monthly meetings where team members provide updates on projects, allowing for realignment if needed. These check-ins ensure that everyone is on the same page and that any potential obstacles can be addressed early. This regularity fosters a shared sense of responsibility, as each person knows they'll have an opportunity to communicate progress.

Creating Space for Open Dialogue in Personal Relationships: In personal relationships, regular check-ins can be casual conversations where each person shares thoughts on how the relationship is progressing, discusses expectations, and reviews how well each is meeting those expectations. This proactive approach allows for minor adjustments before misunderstandings arise, helping both individuals feel heard and supported.

Addressing Challenges in a Constructive Manner: These check-ins provide an avenue for discussing challenges without feeling accusatory. If a commitment hasn't been met, the check-in allows both parties to assess the reasons and find constructive solutions. This encourages problem-solving and reinforces that accountability is a shared goal rather than a judgment.

Regular check-ins help to **normalize accountability** within the relationship, creating a rhythm where trust and communication flow freely. These structured interactions build a sense of reliability and help ensure that everyone is working toward shared goals.

Use Positive Reinforcement

Verification doesn't need to feel confrontational or critical. **Positive reinforcement** allows us to acknowledge and appreciate consistent follow-through, which, in turn, strengthens trust. Recognizing and celebrating reliability fosters a supportive atmosphere where accountability is encouraged and respected.

Reinforcing Reliable Behavior with Recognition: Acknowledging someone's consistent efforts reinforces their motivation to maintain accountability. In a mentorship relationship, for example, praising a mentee for regularly meeting their goals not only shows appreciation but encourages continued effort. Positive reinforcement signals that their accountability is noticed and valued.

Encouraging Growth and Development: In professional settings, acknowledging achievements and consistency reinforces a culture of growth. Positive feedback can be given publicly or privately, depending on what feels most supportive. This type of encouragement creates a feedback loop where accountability feels rewarding, building confidence and reinforcing commitment.

Fostering a Culture of Appreciation: Expressing gratitude for someone's reliability promotes a positive atmosphere that feels mutually supportive. In personal relationships, a simple "Thank you for always being there when I need you" reminds the other person that their efforts are appreciated. This reinforces a bond based on gratitude and trust, making accountability a naturally fulfilling part of the relationship.

Positive reinforcement transforms accountability from a task into a source of **personal fulfillment and connection**. It shows that each person's efforts are respected and that mutual accountability is a valued aspect of the relationship.

Encourage a Culture of Transparency

Transparency is a foundation for trust, and when verification is **practiced openly**, it becomes a normal, accepted part of the relationship. Transparency helps to avoid misunderstandings by aligning expectations from the start, emphasizing that accountability is a mutual responsibility designed to protect the relationship and ensure shared goals are met.

Setting Clear Expectations Early On: By discussing verification practices at the beginning, both parties understand that transparency is an essential component of the relationship. In a business partnership, for example, establishing expectations for regular updates and shared access to project details avoids assumptions. This clarity helps both parties feel secure in knowing that accountability is expected and appreciated.

Creating Open Channels for Feedback and Concerns: Transparency means that both parties are comfortable addressing issues as they arise. If something goes off course, an open channel of communication allows it to be addressed without secrecy or frustration. This approach ensures that verification doesn't feel like surveillance but as a safeguard that benefits both parties.

Fostering Mutual Growth and Development: When accountability is discussed openly, it reinforces that verification is a tool for improvement rather than judgment. Both parties can see verification as a chance to measure progress and refine their contributions. This openness encourages a culture where feedback is welcomed and trust is actively maintained.

Establishing a culture of transparency creates an **environment of mutual respect** and trust, where verification becomes a tool for growth rather than a source of scrutiny. It aligns both parties around a shared commitment to honesty, fostering a relationship that is resilient and built on open communication.

Why Collaborative Accountability Protects and Strengthens Trust

Verification, when approached as a collaborative effort, ensures accountability without compromising the relationship's integrity. By creating a partnership around shared responsibility, both parties remain **aligned and committed to meeting shared expectations**. Collaborative accountability transforms trust from a passive feeling into an active, mutual practice that's maintained over time.

Protecting Trust by Reducing Uncertainty: Collaborative accountability clarifies expectations, reducing the potential for misunderstandings and disappointment. When both parties know what to expect, they're less likely to experience frustration or resentment, preserving the integrity of the relationship.

Building Long-Term Stability Through Accountability: Trust grounded in accountability is better equipped to handle challenges and withstand the test of time. By verifying actions and reinforcing trust through consistency, relationships gain stability, making them more resilient to fluctuations or conflicts.

Ensuring a Balanced Approach to Verification: Collaborative accountability avoids the risk of excessive skepticism, as both parties actively participate in maintaining trust. By sharing responsibility, neither party feels unduly scrutinized, and the relationship remains respectful and balanced.

Approaching verification as a **shared responsibility** reinforces that accountability is not a burden but a commitment that strengthens trust and respect. In this way, verification serves as a foundation that protects the integrity of relationships, ensuring they remain aligned, reliable, and built on mutual respect.

Tools and Techniques for Setting Up Trust Check-Ins, Transparency Protocols, and Accountability Measures

Building a reliable verification process requires practical tools and techniques that make accountability measures **effective, respectful, and supportive**. Structured verification enhances trust by providing clear, consistent, and open pathways for maintaining commitments. Here are strategies for setting up **trust check-ins, transparency protocols, and accountability measures** that help reationships flourish.

Trust Check-Ins

Trust check-ins are **scheduled opportunities** for both parties to evaluate how well expectations are being met, discuss any issues, and adjust agreements if necessary. These check-ins allow for open communication, mutual feedback, and proactive adjustments, reinforcing accountability and ensuring trust remains dynamic and responsive to the relationship's needs.

Schedule Regular Check-Ins: The frequency of check-ins should suit the relationship's context—weekly, monthly, or quarterly. In a work project, weekly check-ins enable team members to share updates, identify potential obstacles, and realign goals as needed. In a personal relationship, monthly or quarterly check-ins might be sufficient for discussing expectations and shared goals, ensuring each person feels heard and valued.

Create a Safe Environment for Feedback: For check-ins to be productive, both parties need to feel safe sharing their thoughts constructively. Set the tone by encouraging respectful and open dialogue, emphasizing that feedback should focus on solutions rather than blame. This approach fosters a positive environment where both parties feel supported in expressing their needs.

Document Progress and Adjust as Needed: During each check-in, document what has been accomplished and note any areas where adjustments may be necessary. This documentation provides a tangible record of progress and allows both parties to reflect on how trust has developed over time. In professional contexts, a project management tool like Trello or Asana can serve as a centralized place to track updates and document discussions.

By creating a **framework of regular accountability**, trust check-ins foster open communication, making trust a dynamic, evolving aspect of the relationship. This structured approach keeps trust active, adaptable, and responsive to changes or new goals.

Transparency Protocols

Transparency protocols provide guidelines for **how information is shared**, ensuring that all parties have access to the details they need to build and maintain trust. These protocols emphasize clarity and openness, reducing misunderstandings and fostering a culture of shared responsibility and mutual understanding.

Establish Clear Communication Standards: Define how often information should be shared and through which channels. For example, in a business relationship, regular updates through a shared project management tool or weekly emails help keep everyone informed. In a personal relationship, weekly or monthly check-ins via messaging or in-person meetings might be effective. Establishing these standards ensures that both parties know when and where to expect updates.

Set Expectations for Disclosure: Determine which information needs to be shared openly, especially when dealing with confidential or sensitive topics. For instance, in community organizations, transparency around decision-making processes might be essential to ensure all members feel included and respected. Setting clear disclosure expectations fosters trust by making sure no party feels blindsided.

Use Shared Platforms for Accountability: Technology can streamline transparency and keep everyone on the same page. Shared platforms like Google Workspace, Asana, or Slack allow parties to **track progress, document updates, and verify task completion** in real time. These tools provide a centralized space for sharing documents, tracking milestones, and maintaining a clear record of commitments.

Transparency protocols help create a structure for **clear, accessible communication** that reduces potential misunderstandings. By keeping everyone informed in a consistent and open manner, these protocols support trust without creating an environment of suspicion.

Accountability Measures

Accountability measures are **formal structures** that help uphold commitments and reinforce responsibility within the relationship. These measures support trust by ensuring that actions align with agreed-upon expectations and provide a framework for addressing unmet commitments or breaches of trust.

Define Consequences for Breaches: Set clear consequences if commitments aren't met. For instance, in a professional setting, missed deadlines could result in adjusting roles or revisiting timelines. In personal relationships, breaches of confidentiality or broken promises might lead to a discussion on boundaries and expectations. Establishing these consequences early on clarifies the importance of accountability and outlines steps to restore trust if it's compromised.

Create Milestones or Progress Markers: Breaking down larger commitments into smaller, measurable milestones allows for more frequent verification of progress. For example, in a long-term project, setting monthly deliverables enables both parties to check progress and make adjustments as needed. In personal commitments, such as fitness goals or shared financial plans, setting weekly check-ins or small goals reinforces commitment and provides regular opportunities to celebrate success.

Formalize Agreements with Contracts or Written Agreements: In professional or legal settings, formal agreements clarify each party's responsibilities, creating a clear basis for verification. Even in informal partnerships, written agreements can provide a reference point to avoid misunderstandings. This might include documented agreements for project deadlines, joint ventures, or shared financial goals, ensuring that all terms are clearly understood and agreed upon.

Accountability measures reinforce **commitment and responsibility** within the relationship, providing a clear and tangible basis for building trust. By breaking down goals, formalizing agreements, and outlining consequences, accountability measures ensure that trust is rooted in observable actions and clear expectations.

Putting These Tools and Techniques Together

Incorporating trust check-ins, transparency protocols, and accountability measures creates a **comprehensive framework** for trust that is proactive, transparent, and mutually beneficial. Each tool serves to strengthen trust through consistent, respectful, and supportive practices, ensuring that accountability enhances rather than undermines the relationship.

Together, these practices help:

Normalize Accountability: By regularly verifying commitments through structured practices, accountability becomes an accepted part of the relationship rather than a sign of mistrust.

Empower Open Communication: These tools create opportunities for open, constructive dialogue about expectations, progress, and any potential concerns, reducing misunderstandings and strengthening trust.

Reinforce Mutual Respect and Responsibility: Each party takes ownership of their commitments, fostering a relationship where trust is actively maintained through consistency and shared responsibility.

By implementing these tools and techniques, trust becomes a **collaborative, evolving process** where both parties contribute to its growth and stability. This structured approach to verification ensures that trust remains strong, adaptable, and aligned with the values and goals of everyone involved.

The Transformative Power of Verification in Building Trust

Verification is a powerful tool that **transforms trust from a simple assumption into a lasting, resilient foundation**. Rather than relying on a passive belief that trust will endure, verification allows us to **actively nurture and reinforce trust** through consistent, observable actions. This approach turns doubt into a constructive force that strengthens the relationship, allowing trust to evolve in a way that is reliable, robust, and deeply grounded in accountability.

Turning Doubt into Constructive Assurance

In most relationships, a natural level of doubt or caution is present, especially in early stages. Verification transforms this doubt from a potential barrier into a **positive catalyst for trust**. Instead of allowing doubt to undermine the relationship, verification harnesses it as a tool for clarity and assurance. By creating opportunities for confirmation, we turn uncertainty into a constructive element that helps build a solid foundation.

Bridging Gaps in New Relationships: In new relationships, whether personal or professional, verification enables us to bridge gaps by establishing a track record of reliability. For example, when a new business partner consistently delivers on small promises or meets deadlines, verification helps turn initial doubts into confidence. This process is especially valuable in high-stakes relationships where a strong foundation of trust is crucial for long-term success.

Reinforcing Trust in Established Relationships: In longstanding relationships, verification keeps trust alive and dynamic. Even in relationships built over years, small gestures of accountability—like following through on agreed tasks or regularly updating each other on shared goals—help ensure that trust is not taken for granted. Verification in this context serves as a reminder that trust is continually valued and maintained.

Verification turns **doubt into an opportunity for growth**, transforming it from a source of anxiety to a way to deepen and fortify trust.

Creating a Resilient, Adaptable Relationship Dynamic

Verification makes trust **resilient and adaptable**. By setting up structured check-ins, transparency protocols, and accountability measures, we turn trust into an ongoing process that can withstand challenges. Trust becomes dynamic, evolving as the relationship progresses, and adapting to new circumstances or changing needs. This adaptability is essential for relationships to thrive over time.

Providing Stability During Change: As circumstances change—whether due to shifting goals, new challenges, or external pressures—verification helps maintain stability within the relationship. For example, in a business relationship undergoing a major project transition, regular check-ins and progress updates ensure that both parties remain aligned, even if the work's scope or focus shifts. This adaptability reinforces that trust is not contingent on conditions staying the same but can evolve to meet new demands.

Enhancing Flexibility in Personal Relationships: In personal relationships, verification enables us to adjust trust as people's lives and needs change. When partners regularly discuss expectations, goals, and boundaries, they're able to adapt to life's ebbs and flows—such as career changes, moves, or new family responsibilities. Verification in this way turns trust into a **living part of the relationship**, making it responsive to real-world complexities.

By making trust resilient and adaptable, verification **ensures that trust can endure change** rather than being weakened by it. This adaptability allows relationships to grow stronger even in the face of uncertainty.

Turning Trust into an Active, Ongoing Process

Verification reframes trust as an active process rather than a passive assumption. Instead of hoping that trust will stay intact, we actively work to **build and sustain it**. Every action taken in alignment with the conditions of trust reinforces the relationship, making it more resilient to misunderstandings, conflicts, and external pressures.

Supporting Long-Term Commitment: In both personal and professional relationships, verification encourages a commitment to long-term consistency. When each party is accountable for their promises and routinely demonstrates their reliability, trust is continually renewed. This active reinforcement prevents trust from fading over time, ensuring it remains a reliable element of the relationship.

Encouraging Proactive Conflict Resolution: Verification helps address potential issues early on, allowing for proactive conflict resolution. By checking in regularly and maintaining transparency, misunderstandings can be cleared up before they escalate into larger problems. This habit of early intervention strengthens trust by creating a culture of openness and accountability.

Through verification, trust becomes an **ongoing commitment**—a conscious choice sustained by effort, respect, and transparent communication. Rather than assuming trust will endure, we actively invest in it, keeping it alive and healthy.

Verification as an Enhancer, Not a Detractor of Trust

Contrary to the misconception that verification might diminish trust, it actually enhances it by making trust **real and tangible**. Verification turns trust into something measurable, grounded in the actions and decisions of those involved. Far from eroding trust, this practice solidifies it, creating a structure that supports and nurtures the relationship.

Building Trust Through Evidence, Not Assumptions: When trust is reinforced by actions that align with words, it becomes much more meaningful. Verification provides a foundation of evidence, helping us to rely on people because we have seen consistent proof of their commitment. This evidence-based trust is more reliable and less susceptible to disillusionment than trust built solely on assumptions or hopes.

Making Trust Sustainable Over Time: Verification prevents the erosion of trust by making it sustainable. Without verification, trust may wane over time as assumptions lead to potential misunderstandings or unmet expectations. Verification, however, keeps trust grounded in reality, ensuring it can grow and deepen over time without the risk of becoming fragile or taken for granted.

Verification doesn't detract from trust; it **elevates it by rooting it in reality**. By making trust something that can be observed and reinforced, verification ensures that trust remains strong, stable, and enduring.

Building Relationships That Thrive on Accountability

The transformative power of verification lies in its ability to foster **relationships built on mutual accountability**. Structured check-ins, transparency protocols, and accountability measures create a collaborative environment where each party feels a shared responsibility for maintaining trust. This approach fosters relationships that are not only reliable but also empowering, as each person understands their role in building and sustaining trust.

Empowering Both Parties to Take Ownership of Trust: Verification empowers both parties to actively participate in maintaining trust. When each person understands the expectations and contributes to the accountability process, they feel a greater sense of ownership over the relationship's success. This shared responsibility fosters a balanced relationship where trust is mutual and collaborative.

Reinforcing Mutual Respect and Commitment: Accountability measures emphasize respect, as they show that each party is valued and that their commitments are taken seriously. By establishing clear expectations and following through with consistent actions, both parties reinforce their dedication to the relationship. This mutual respect further strengthens trust, making it more resilient to challenges.

The active, collaborative nature of verification ensures that trust is **reinforced through mutual effort**. Relationships that thrive on accountability become stronger, more transparent, and deeply rooted in shared goals and values.

Making Trust a Tangible, Enduring Force

Verification transforms trust into something **tangible, measurable, and enduring**. By setting up check-ins, transparency protocols, and accountability measures, we shift trust from a fragile assumption into a powerful, long-lasting force. Verification ensures that trust remains robust, adaptable, and resilient, capable of weathering change and evolving over time.

As we make trust an **active process**, each verification becomes a step toward a more profound connection. Trust is no longer just a passive feeling; it becomes an intentional choice reinforced by actions, respect, and shared accountability. This approach fosters relationships that are deeply satisfying, fulfilling, and capable of withstanding the complexities of modern life.

In summary, verification doesn't weaken trust—it makes it real. It is the commitment to aligning actions with promises, creating a foundation of trust that stands the test of time. Through verification, we build relationships that are **rooted in integrity, strengthened by transparency, and resilient through accountability**, transforming trust into an enduring and powerful connection.

Embracing Accountability as a Key Component of Trust

Accountability is at the heart of meaningful, enduring trust. **Embracing accountability** as a core element in relationships allows us to approach trust with **clarity, openness, and confidence**. Rather than passively assuming that trust will endure, accountability encourages both parties to take an active role in nurturing, maintaining, and upholding trust. This approach transforms trust from a static feeling into a dynamic commitment, where clear expectations and aligned actions strengthen the connection.

Making Trust an Active Commitment

When we prioritize accountability in trust, we **move from a passive to an active stance**. Trust is no longer something we assume will exist indefinitely; instead, it becomes an ongoing commitment that both parties consciously work to uphold. Accountability means that trust isn't just a matter of believing in someone—it's about making sure that belief is consistently supported by actions.

Engaging Both Sides in Building Trust: Accountability encourages both parties to contribute actively to the trust-building process. This collaboration creates a balanced dynamic where each person takes ownership of their role in maintaining trust. For instance, in a friendship, accountability might involve consistently keeping promises, being there in times of need, and openly addressing any misunderstandings. Each action strengthens the connection, making trust something that both parties continually invest in.

Reinforcing Trust Through Regular Actions: Accountability brings trust out of the abstract and into the tangible. Regular actions, such as meeting commitments, showing up on time, and following through on promises, reinforce trust by making it visible. Each consistent action serves as evidence that trust is being honored, reducing the risk of doubt and reinforcing a sense of security within the relationship.

By turning trust into an **active, reciprocal process**, accountability empowers both parties to take responsibility for the relationship's well-being, creating a foundation of mutual respect and shared commitment.

Creating Clarity and Confidence through Verification

Accountability provides clarity and reassurance, transforming trust into a **clear and confident expectation**. When verification is integrated into trust-building, expectations are clearly defined, reducing misunderstandings and promoting openness. Verification is not about doubting the other person; it's about aligning actions with expectations, which helps both parties feel secure and confident in their connection.

Defining and Aligning Expectations: Embracing accountability involves setting clear expectations from the start. For example, in a work relationship, accountability might mean outlining specific responsibilities, deadlines, and quality standards for a project. This clarity removes ambiguity and sets a standard for what trust looks like in that context. Each party knows what is expected, making it easier to meet those expectations and avoid potential conflicts.

Building Confidence through Consistency: When both parties regularly demonstrate accountability, it strengthens confidence. Consistently meeting expectations—whether by being reliable, transparent, or communicative—reinforces trust by showing that each person can count on the other. This consistency creates a steady rhythm within the relationship, where trust feels dependable and deeply rooted.

Verification allows us to approach trust with confidence and security, knowing that our expectations are supported by tangible actions. Accountability, therefore, **eliminates guesswork** from trust, transforming it into a reliable force based on mutual understanding and aligned values.

Trust as a Reliable, Enduring Force

Accountability transforms trust into a **reliable, enduring force**. With verification as part of the process, trust becomes more than just a feeling—it becomes an ongoing commitment marked by observable actions and shared values. When trust is built through accountability, it's not easily shaken by temporary conflicts or misunderstandings; instead, it's grounded in a pattern of mutual respect and dependability.

Strengthening Relationships Against Adversity: Trust that's built on accountability is more resilient in the face of challenges. In times of adversity, accountability provides a framework for navigating difficulties. For example, in a long-term partnership, financial strains or career changes can test trust. However, if both partners maintain accountability—through transparency, proactive communication, and a willingness to address challenges together—trust remains strong and resilient.

Making Trust Sustainable over Time: Trust is most sustainable when it's reinforced by accountability. Relationships where accountability is a priority are less likely to experience trust breakdowns because trust is not assumed or taken for granted. Instead, it's actively supported by consistent, responsible actions over time. This sustainability is key in relationships that need to endure through life's changes, as accountability ensures that trust can grow and adapt.

Accountability turns trust into a **stable, lasting foundation** that can withstand the ups and downs of life. It shifts trust from a fragile, uncertain feeling into a resilient force that each person can rely on, no matter the circumstances.

Verification as a Bridge Between Expectations and Reality

Verification serves as a bridge, connecting **expectations with reality**. Rather than viewing verification as a barrier to trust, we can embrace it as a tool that grounds trust in reality, ensuring that it's based on clear, consistent actions. This bridge enables us to build trust that's both meaningful and measurable, making it a cornerstone of healthy, fulfilling relationships.

Ensuring Trust Reflects Real Interactions: Verification brings expectations into alignment with real-world behavior. For example, in a team setting, periodic performance reviews provide an opportunity to ensure that everyone is meeting their commitments, promoting a culture of accountability and trust. These reviews are not about questioning competence but about celebrating achievements and addressing any gaps in a constructive way. This ensures that trust in each team member is well-placed, supported by evidence of their contribution.

Reinforcing Accountability with Clear Feedback: Verification offers a pathway for constructive feedback, allowing both parties to address any misalignments between expectations and actions. In personal relationships, for instance, discussing unmet expectations with openness and respect reinforces accountability without fostering resentment. Verification allows both individuals to feel secure that any issues can be addressed openly, keeping trust strong and transparent.

Verification is not about creating barriers; it's about building bridges that **connect intentions with outcomes**. This alignment transforms trust into a tangible, real experience, making it something that both parties can see, measure, and strengthen over time.

The Empowering Effect of Accountability in Trust

Embracing accountability as a key component of trust empowers us to **take control of our relationships**. It fosters a sense of security, respect, and active engagement, making trust something we actively build and protect. Accountability ensures that trust is based on respect and responsibility, empowering both parties to feel valued, involved, and committed.

Promoting Empowerment Through Mutual Respect: Accountability encourages each party to take ownership of their role in the relationship, promoting a balance of power where each person's efforts are respected. This mutual respect makes trust a source of strength, as it's not one-sided but actively supported by both parties.

Encouraging Continuous Growth and Improvement: Accountability allows trust to be dynamic and responsive to growth. By holding each other accountable, both parties are encouraged to evolve, improve, and strive for consistency in their actions. For example, in a professional mentorship, accountability ensures that the mentee is meeting goals and making progress, while the mentor is fulfilling their role as a supportive guide. This dynamic approach fosters growth, development, and a sense of shared accomplishment.

The accountability approach to trust **reinforces a sense of agency and shared purpose**. It encourages each person to invest in the relationship actively, creating a relationship where trust is nurtured, protected, and continually valued.

Transforming Trust into a Measurable, Lasting Connection

By integrating accountability into our approach to trust, we create relationships that are capable of flourishing in a complex, uncertain world. Verification and accountability don't detract from trust; they elevate it, making it something we can rely on, measure, and actively engage with. This approach empowers us to **build connections that are both meaningful and lasting**.

In a world where change and uncertainty are constant, trust supported by accountability becomes a vital resource. It allows relationships to thrive, adapt, and grow in a way that is mutually beneficial and deeply satisfying. Accountability ensures that trust is never static or assumed—it's an ongoing, shared commitment that reflects the highest level of respect, integrity, and mutual investment.

As we embrace accountability as a core component of trust, we transform trust into a **real, sustainable foundation** that enhances our relationships, making them stronger, more resilient, and ready to meet the challenges and joys of life together.

5: The Spectrum of Trust and Doubt—Finding Your Balance

Trust is not a one-size-fits-all approach, nor does it always exist in a binary state of full confidence or complete mistrust. Instead, trust and doubt operate along a **spectrum** that varies depending on context, past experiences, and the nature of each relationship. In this chapter, we'll introduce the **trust-doubt spectrum** as a framework to help you navigate trust across different settings, recognize when and how much doubt might be appropriate, and find the balance that feels right for you.

This spectrum isn't about fostering distrust but about allowing a **thoughtful blend of trust and caution** to guide your relationships in a way that feels secure, adaptive, and authentic.

Understanding the Trust-Doubt Spectrum

The trust-doubt spectrum is a **flexible framework** that allows us to assess and adjust our levels of trust in various contexts. Trust is not static; it shifts according to factors such as past experiences, the stakes involved, and the reliability of the individuals or organizations we engage with. This spectrum ranges from **high trust**, marked by open confidence, to **high doubt**, where caution and skepticism take precedence. Navigating this spectrum thoughtfully helps us make informed choices about where we feel secure and where we may need to protect ourselves.

The trust-doubt spectrum is not about promoting distrust; rather, it encourages us to find a **balanced approach to trust** that aligns with our experiences and needs in each relationship. By situating ourselves appropriately along this continuum, we can engage authentically and protect our boundaries, adapting our levels of trust based on what we observe and experience.

Levels of Trust on the Spectrum

Each level on the trust-doubt spectrum serves a unique purpose, with each degree of trust or doubt offering **specific advantages** depending on the context. Understanding these distinctions allows us to approach relationships thoughtfully, matching our trust to the realities of each situation.

High Trust: Open Confidence

At the high-trust end of the spectrum, we experience **open confidence with minimal doubt**. This level of trust is typically found in relationships with a long history of consistent, reliable behavior. High trust involves vulnerability and a sense of security, as we feel confident that the other person has our best interests at heart.

Characteristics of High Trust: This level is characterized by comfort in being open and vulnerable, a willingness to share personal information or rely on the other person, and an absence of significant caution or skepticism. We allow ourselves to rely on the relationship without hesitation, knowing that past experiences have proven it to be stable and trustworthy.

Examples of High Trust Relationships: Relationships with close friends, long-term partners, or family members often reside in this high-trust zone. For example, a friend you've known and trusted for years is someone you can be vulnerable with, share sensitive details, and depend on in times of need. Similarly, in a long-term romantic relationship, high trust allows partners to openly share fears, dreams, and insecurities, confident in the stability of the connection.

Benefits and Risks: High trust fosters deep connection and intimacy, as we feel secure in being fully authentic without the need for protective barriers. However, high trust also comes with vulnerability; if this trust is betrayed, the sense of betrayal can be profound. This level of trust is best reserved for those who have consistently shown themselves to be reliable and aligned with our values.

Moderate Trust with Caution: Balanced Engagement

Moderate trust with caution represents a **balanced, thoughtful approach to trust.** This midpoint is ideal for relationships where we feel confident in certain areas but recognize that some aspects still require boundaries or protective measures. Here, we engage openly while maintaining a level of awareness, ensuring that we don't overextend our trust.

Characteristics of Moderate Trust with Caution: This level of trust includes a layer of engagement alongside a degree of reservation. While we may trust the person or organization for certain tasks or information, we still refrain from full vulnerability. This approach allows us to be connected while staying aware of the need for discernment.

Examples of Moderate Trust Relationships: In professional relationships, for example, you might trust a coworker to handle day-to-day responsibilities but may choose to keep certain personal or sensitive information private until there's more experience working together. Similarly, in a new friendship, you may share interests or attend social gatherings together while waiting to see how they handle deeper, more personal conversations.

Benefits and Risks: Moderate trust with caution enables us to engage meaningfully while protecting areas of vulnerability. It provides the flexibility to build trust over time and to adjust boundaries as the relationship develops. The primary risk is that it may inhibit full connection initially, but this caution can be beneficial as the relationship unfolds and proves its reliability.

High Doubt: Trust with Skepticism and Caution

At the high-doubt end of the spectrum, **skepticism and caution take precedence**. This approach is appropriate in relationships or settings where the potential for risk is high, or where there is limited information about the person's or organization's reliability. High doubt allows us to remain engaged with a focus on protecting ourselves, ensuring that trust is built incrementally and is always accompanied by a level of verification.

Characteristics of High Doubt: High doubt involves a cautious stance where we require evidence of reliability before extending trust. This approach includes setting strict boundaries, verifying actions before reliance, and maintaining a healthy degree of skepticism. High doubt serves as a form of self-protection, enabling us to observe and assess behavior without overcommitting.

Examples of High-Doubt Relationships: This approach is common in unfamiliar or high-stakes environments, such as entering a business partnership with someone new or investing in a project with a potentially high return but unknown risks. In these cases, you might trust certain aspects of the partnership (like the viability of the project) but withhold full trust until a track record is established.

Benefits and Risks: High doubt protects us from unnecessary vulnerability, allowing us to engage without risking a major breach of trust. This approach is useful for risk management, especially in new or high-stakes situations. However, high doubt can create distance in relationships if it's not gradually adjusted as trust is earned. Being overly cautious may prevent the development of deeper connections, so it's essential to allow room for growth as trust is demonstrated.

The Adaptive Flexibility of the Trust-Doubt Spectrum

Each level on the trust-doubt spectrum has its **purpose and place** in our relationships, allowing us to adapt our approach to trust depending on the situation, context, and individuals involved. Rather than viewing trust as an all-or-nothing state, this spectrum provides the flexibility to **move between levels** of trust and doubt based on our needs, experiences, and the actions of others.

Adapting Trust Across Contexts: In personal relationships, we may naturally fall toward the high-trust end with those who've proven reliable and supportive over time, while professional relationships may call for moderate trust with caution. In unfamiliar or uncertain settings, embracing high doubt initially allows us to protect ourselves until we have more information. Adapting trust across different contexts ensures that our approach is relevant to each unique situation.

Moving Along the Spectrum: Trust and doubt are fluid and responsive, meaning they can increase or decrease as relationships develop. If a coworker demonstrates consistent reliability, we may find ourselves moving from moderate trust with caution to a higher level of trust. Conversely, if someone fails to meet commitments or breaks trust, we might shift toward higher doubt to protect ourselves.

Creating Space for Gradual Trust-Building: This spectrum also makes room for gradual trust-building. Relationships can progress naturally without feeling pressure to reach full trust prematurely. Each step along the spectrum allows us to test reliability, adjust expectations, and create a foundation of trust based on consistent, verifiable behavior.

The trust-doubt spectrum empowers us to **tailor our level of trust** to each relationship, adapting as we go, and avoiding extremes of blind trust or rigid suspicion. This balanced approach respects the complexity of human relationships, helping us engage meaningfully while protecting our boundaries.

By embracing the trust-doubt spectrum, we can approach trust as a flexible, adaptive tool that aligns with our personal experiences and the unique demands of each relationship. This perspective enables us to honor both our need for connection and our right to self-protection, allowing us to build trust in a way that is **intentional, resilient, and deeply fulfilling**.

How to Navigate Varying Levels of Doubt

Doubt isn't inherently negative; when used thoughtfully, it becomes a **powerful tool** for building trust responsibly. Different situations call for varying levels of doubt, ranging from mild skepticism to high caution. Recognizing where you are on the **trust-doubt spectrum** in each relationship enables you to approach trust in a balanced, realistic, and self-protective way. By choosing the appropriate level of doubt, you can build trust that's secure, adaptable, and respectful of each relationship's unique complexities.

Mild Skepticism: Trust with a Touch of Vigilance

Mild skepticism is useful in relationships that are **new or developing**, where trust is present but hasn't been fully tested. This level of doubt doesn't prevent trust but instead encourages you to remain observant, allowing trust to grow gradually as it's earned. Mild skepticism serves as a gentle reminder to be alert while staying open to new connections and experiences.

Example Setting: In a new friendship, you might be open to spending time together and sharing interests but choose to hold back on deeply personal disclosures until you feel more secure in the connection. By maintaining mild skepticism, you allow trust to develop naturally, based on shared experiences rather than assumptions.

Practical Approach: **Trust actions over words** by observing the other person's consistency and responsiveness over time. Are they dependable? Do they follow through on what they say? Mild skepticism helps you pace the growth of trust while allowing positive experiences to reinforce it. If a new friend consistently shows up and respects boundaries, for example, your level of trust will naturally increase over time.

Benefits: Mild skepticism allows for genuine engagement while protecting against premature vulnerability. By pacing the development of trust, you can deepen the connection at a comfortable rate, feeling more secure as trust is earned. This approach also helps avoid the disappointment that can arise from extending too much trust too quickly.

Mild skepticism encourages **mindful engagement**, allowing you to build trust gradually without sacrificing openness. It provides a gentle buffer that allows you to observe the other person's actions and intentions before fully investing in the relationship.

Moderate Caution: Trust with Defined Boundaries

Moderate caution is suitable in situations where **conditional trust** is needed, with specific boundaries that help you maintain control and avoid unnecessary risks. This level of doubt allows you to engage meaningfully with others while protecting your interests by establishing clear limits. Moderate caution is often appropriate for professional relationships, new partnerships, or situations where the stakes are moderate but meaningful.

Example Setting: In a professional context, you might trust a colleague to handle day-to-day tasks while reserving sensitive information or strategic decision-making power for yourself. This approach encourages collaboration without the vulnerability that comes from placing full trust in a developing relationship.

Practical Approach: **Define boundaries clearly and communicate them openly**. For example, if you're working with a colleague on a project, you might agree on specific areas where they have autonomy while retaining oversight on certain critical aspects. Set boundaries that reflect your comfort level and clearly convey expectations to the other party. This way, each person knows their responsibilities, and trust is managed without ambiguity.

Benefits: Moderate caution protects you from overextending trust while allowing you to develop a working relationship. By establishing clear boundaries, you avoid misunderstandings, set healthy limits, and create a safe space for trust to grow as reliability is proven. This level of caution ensures that trust is extended in a way that is **both thoughtful and adaptive**, making it easier to adjust as the relationship evolves.

Moderate caution allows for **secure, structured engagement** in relationships where complete trust might not be warranted initially. This balanced approach to trust enables meaningful connection while respecting personal boundaries and promoting clarity.

High Caution: Trust with Verification

High caution involves **trusting selectively**, using structured measures like verification or checks to ensure accountability. This level of doubt is essential in high-stakes situations or relationships where trust hasn't yet been earned, such as business partnerships, financial transactions, or new collaborations. High caution allows you to minimize risk by requiring concrete proof of reliability before placing full trust.

Example Setting: When working with a new contractor on a significant project, you might trust their skills but opt to verify progress through milestones and check-ins. For instance, you might structure payments in phases, with each payment contingent on verified progress. High caution ensures that you're not overly vulnerable and that the contractor's performance aligns with agreed-upon standards.

Practical Approach: **Use accountability measures** like formal agreements, regular updates, or third-party oversight. Structured verification enables you to trust gradually, based on evidence and accountability rather than assumptions. In high-stakes scenarios, this approach turns doubt into a proactive form of risk management. For example, in a new business venture, conducting background checks, setting up regular progress reviews, and agreeing on written contracts ensures that trust is earned over time.

Benefits: High caution is protective, allowing you to engage without the risk of blind trust. It provides a framework for verifying actions before committing fully, helping you manage expectations and avoid disappointment or loss. While high caution may initially limit emotional connection, it's an effective strategy for building trust incrementally based on consistent, reliable behavior.

High caution fosters **trust with security and resilience**, allowing you to navigate complex relationships with confidence. By structuring trust through verification, you minimize vulnerability while still leaving space for trust to grow.

Each Level of Doubt as a Tool for Setting Boundaries and Pacing Trust

Each level of doubt on the trust-doubt spectrum is a tool that helps set boundaries, pace trust, and engage responsibly. Consciously choosing your level of doubt in any relationship empowers you to protect your interests and adapt to the unique dynamics of each connection.

Flexibility and Adaptation: Recognizing where you fall on the spectrum for each relationship enables you to move between levels of doubt as the relationship progresses. For example, if a new colleague consistently demonstrates reliability, you might shift from moderate caution to a more open level of trust, adjusting boundaries to match their proven trustworthiness.

Building a Foundation for Long-Term Trust: Using these levels of doubt thoughtfully allows you to develop trust as a **gradual, layered process**. Each stage of doubt, from mild skepticism to high caution, provides a structured foundation for trust to grow at a natural pace, creating a more resilient relationship.

Maintaining Control and Protecting Well-Being: By situating yourself appropriately along the trust-doubt spectrum, you take control of your emotional and practical investments. This ensures that you're not overextended in relationships that may not yet warrant full trust, helping you maintain a sense of security and well-being.

Navigating varying levels of doubt equips you with a **balanced, adaptive approach to trust**, making it easier to build meaningful connections while honoring your needs and limits. This spectrum of doubt enables you to tailor your level of trust according to the nature of each relationship, empowering you to engage mindfully and responsibly.

By embracing doubt as a constructive aspect of trust, you create a framework that's adaptable, realistic, and protective. Each level of doubt serves a unique purpose, enabling you to build trust in a way that is resilient, self-aware, and deeply fulfilling.

Self-Assessment: Where Do You Stand on the Spectrum of Trust?

This self-assessment helps you identify your natural tendencies on the **trust-doubt spectrum** across various types of relationships. By examining your approach to trust in different settings, you can better understand where you feel most comfortable on the spectrum and how you might adjust your level of trust or doubt to enhance your well-being and relational health. Use the following questions to reflect on your approach to trust in personal, professional, and community settings.

Personal Relationships

In personal relationships, trust often runs deep, and our approaches to doubt can vary based on past experiences, personal values, and comfort with vulnerability. Reflecting on your patterns with close friends and romantic partners can help you identify whether you tend to extend trust readily or if you take a more cautious approach.

Close Friendships

Do you feel comfortable confiding personal matters without fear of betrayal?

If yes, you may naturally lean toward high trust in friendships, opening up without reservation.

If no, you may tend to keep certain boundaries, choosing to share personal information only with those who have proven trustworthy over time.

Do you need time to observe consistency before feeling fully at ease?

If yes, you may favor moderate trust with a degree of caution, waiting to observe consistent behavior before deepening the relationship.

If no, you might readily extend trust, focusing on openness and connection rather than needing immediate proof of reliability.

How do you react when trust is broken? Do you address it openly, or do you find yourself pulling back?

If you address it openly, you may value direct communication in maintaining trust.

If you pull back, you might find it difficult to reestablish trust once it's been broken, leaning toward high caution after a breach.

Romantic Relationships

How quickly do you tend to trust romantic partners?

If you tend to trust quickly, you may favor high trust in romantic settings, embracing openness early on.

If you take more time, you might be comfortable with moderate trust, allowing the relationship to develop gradually.

Are you open to vulnerability early on, or do you feel more comfortable building trust over time?

If you're open early on, you may not feel the need for doubt and might easily embrace vulnerability.

If you prefer to build trust over time, you likely lean toward moderate caution, balancing connection with a layer of self-protection.

How important are trust-reinforcing actions (like open communication) to feeling secure?

If very important, you likely value accountability in the relationship, leaning toward moderate trust with a need for observable, consistent actions.

If less important, you may prioritize emotional openness over a strict need for accountability, placing a higher value on spontaneous connection.

Professional Relationships

In professional settings, trust is often tied to **accountability and reliability**. Your approach to trust with colleagues and team members may depend on your role, the nature of your work, and the degree of risk or responsibility involved.

Colleagues

Do you generally trust coworkers with responsibilities without supervision, or do you prefer to keep tabs?

If you trust them without supervision, you likely favor moderate to high trust in the workplace, placing confidence in team members' abilities.

If you keep tabs, you may lean toward moderate caution, ensuring that tasks are completed as expected.

How do you handle situations where colleagues don't meet your expectations? Do you give second chances or set stricter boundaries?

If you give second chances, you might lean toward moderate trust, allowing for some flexibility.

If you set stricter boundaries, you likely prefer higher caution, adjusting trust levels based on performance.

Leadership or Management

Are you comfortable delegating tasks fully, or do you prefer regular updates to ensure accountability?

If you delegate fully, you may lean toward high trust in your team, empowering them to take ownership.

If you prefer updates, you might practice moderate caution, ensuring accountability while allowing some independence.

How do you manage trust with team members? Do you allow room for mistakes, or do you expect high reliability from the start?

If you allow room for mistakes, you likely support a culture of growth and might lean toward moderate trust.

If you expect high reliability, you may lean toward high caution, emphasizing consistency and accountability from the outset.

Community and Acquaintance-Level Relationships

With acquaintances and in community settings, trust may be more conditional and influenced by the **nature of the group** and its values. Your comfort level with openness and trust in these settings can vary depending on familiarity and shared goals.

Acquaintances

Do you tend to share openly with new acquaintances, or do you prefer to keep conversations surface-level until you know them better?

If you share openly, you might lean toward moderate trust, embracing connections without needing much assurance.

If you keep things surface-level, you may prefer mild skepticism, allowing trust to develop gradually.

Are you naturally inclined to give the benefit of the doubt, or are you cautious about overextending trust?

If you give the benefit of the doubt, you may favor openness in social interactions, focusing on potential connections over caution.

If you're cautious, you likely value boundaries and might lean toward moderate to high caution, especially in unfamiliar settings.

Community Groups or Clubs

In group settings, do you trust others to uphold shared values and responsibilities, or do you need clear guidelines?

If you trust others to uphold values, you may lean toward moderate trust in communal settings, assuming shared commitment.

If you need clear guidelines, you might prefer moderate caution, ensuring that everyone is aligned before extending full trust.

How do you approach shared responsibilities? Are you open to equal input, or do you feel more comfortable when roles and rules are clearly defined?

If you're open to equal input, you might favor a balanced approach, trusting that others will contribute fairly.

If you prefer defined roles, you likely appreciate accountability and might lean toward moderate to high caution, ensuring roles are clear and expectations met.

Reflection: Finding Your Comfort Level on the Trust-Doubt Spectrum

By reflecting on these questions, you gain insights into your natural tendencies on the trust-doubt spectrum for each type of relationship. Recognizing where you typically stand can help you identify areas where you might adjust your level of trust or doubt to support your well-being.

Adjusting Levels of Trust for Balance: If you find that you often lean heavily toward high trust, consider whether a bit more caution might serve you well in certain relationships, especially new ones. Conversely, if you lean toward high doubt, think about relationships where increasing trust might help you build more meaningful connections.

Understanding Situational Trust: Trust isn't a "one size fits all" approach. You might be comfortable with high trust in personal relationships but prefer moderate caution in professional settings. Knowing this distinction can help you adapt to each context without feeling that you have to trust or doubt uniformly across all areas of life.

Using Doubt as a Protective Measure: If certain relationships leave you feeling uncertain, practicing a higher degree of caution may allow you to feel secure while still engaging. Mild skepticism or moderate caution provides a balanced way to interact without feeling overly vulnerable.

This self-assessment helps you **align your trust levels with the reality of each relationship**, making trust a dynamic and adaptable tool in your personal, professional, and community interactions. By understanding where you stand on the spectrum of trust, you empower yourself to build connections that feel both safe and authentic, ultimately enhancing your well-being and relational health.

Finding Your Personal Balance on the Trust-Doubt Spectrum

Once you understand where you naturally fall on the trust-doubt spectrum, the next step is to **find a comfortable balance** for each unique relationship. Trust and doubt aren't static; they're fluid and should adjust over time in response to changes in behavior, commitment, and context. By adapting your approach as relationships evolve, you allow yourself to **align expectations with reality** and build connections that feel both secure and genuine.

Leaning Toward Trust

In relationships where individuals have consistently proven reliable, it may be beneficial to lean toward trust. **Leaning toward trust** doesn't mean being naive; rather, it's about letting past positive experiences guide a more open and connected approach to the relationship.

Benefits of Leaning Toward Trust: When trust is well-earned, leaning toward openness can enhance intimacy and connection, helping the relationship deepen. Feeling comfortable and secure in the trustworthiness of someone else encourages you to engage more fully, share openly, and rely on the other person for support. In these cases, leaning toward trust can transform relationships, making them richer and more rewarding.

Practical Tips: Reflect on past experiences where the person consistently met your expectations and respected boundaries. In moments of doubt, remind yourself of these positive patterns. Leaning toward trust also means being open to moments of vulnerability, allowing the other person to feel valued and connected. You might choose to share more, let down your guard, or ask for support, knowing you're building on a foundation of proven trust.

Examples: If you have a friend who's always shown up when needed, leaning toward trust allows you to engage without reservation, knowing you can count on them. In a work context, if a colleague has repeatedly demonstrated competence and reliability, trusting them with larger projects or collaborative efforts can strengthen the professional bond and foster teamwork.

Leaning toward trust is a **reward for demonstrated reliability** and allows relationships to flourish with a foundation of confidence and security.

Maintaining Caution

In new or high-stakes relationships, **maintaining caution** is often wise until trust is fully earned. This approach allows you to stay engaged while also setting protective boundaries that prevent unnecessary vulnerability.

Benefits of Maintaining Caution: Caution serves as a natural filter that ensures you're not extending trust prematurely. By building trust gradually, you allow the other person to demonstrate their reliability over time, reducing the risk of betrayal or disappointment. Caution helps you remain present in the relationship while keeping a layer of self-protection in place, allowing trust to grow at a pace that feels comfortable and secure.

Practical Tips: Set boundaries early, and be clear about what you're comfortable sharing or delegating. In conversations, observe consistency between the other person's words and actions, and gradually extend trust as you feel confident. Look for signs of alignment between what the other person says and does, and be mindful of any red flags that suggest the need for more caution.

Examples: In a new romantic relationship, maintaining caution might mean waiting to share deeply personal details until the person has shown they are supportive and trustworthy. In a new business partnership, you might start with small collaborative projects, using milestones and progress checks to ensure accountability before committing to larger ventures.

Maintaining caution creates a **safe space for trust to develop** naturally and allows you to gauge the other person's trustworthiness before becoming deeply invested.

Adjusting as Needed

Trust and doubt aren't fixed; they should **adapt to the evolving dynamics of each relationship**. As circumstances change, it's helpful to adjust your approach up or down the trust-doubt spectrum, ensuring that your level of trust remains in line with the relationship's current reality.

Benefits of Adjusting Trust: By remaining flexible, you allow the relationship to grow and respond to new experiences, changes in behavior, and shifts in context. This adaptability prevents you from being overly trusting when caution is needed or overly skeptical when trust has been earned. Adjusting as needed helps you honor the relationship's evolution while also honoring your own boundaries.

Practical Tips: Periodically reassess the relationship, asking yourself whether your current level of trust aligns with the other person's actions and behaviors. Be willing to dial back trust if new concerns arise or deepen it as the person continues to show reliability. Adjustments can be subtle, such as gradually sharing more over time or setting firmer boundaries when issues arise.

Examples: If a close friend begins to exhibit inconsistent behavior, you might adjust by setting limits on what you share or by addressing the issue openly. Conversely, if a new colleague consistently performs well and meets expectations, you might gradually increase your trust, inviting them to take on more significant responsibilities.

Adjusting trust allows you to **honor changes in the relationship** and ensures that your approach remains responsive and relevant to the current dynamics.

Creating Relationships That Are Safe, Authentic, and Sustainable

By consciously navigating the trust-doubt spectrum, you empower yourself to cultivate relationships that feel both **safe and fulfilling**. This approach is about finding the balance that works best for each connection, building trust in a way that respects the other person while also protecting your emotional well-being.

Balancing Openness with Boundaries: Finding your personal balance means knowing when to be open and when to protect your boundaries. With a friend who has proven loyal and supportive, for instance, you might lean toward full trust, sharing openly and relying on them without hesitation. With new acquaintances or high-stakes connections, moderate caution allows you to participate without exposing yourself to unnecessary risk.

Building Trust Gradually with Clarity and Discernment: By adjusting your approach, you build relationships with a **foundation of clarity and discernment**. Trust is developed at a pace that feels comfortable, strengthening as reliability is shown and respect is maintained. This mindful approach allows you to enjoy connection while ensuring that trust is sustainable and realistic.

Resilience and Adaptability: A balanced approach on the trust-doubt spectrum creates resilience in your relationships. You're able to adapt to challenges, navigate misunderstandings, and maintain trust even through life's inevitable changes. Flexibility in trust keeps relationships dynamic and responsive, able to withstand ups and downs without breaking.

Finding balance on the trust-doubt spectrum helps you create **authentic connections** that reflect your values and needs. You build trust thoughtfully, using a blend of openness, caution, and adaptability, and create relationships that are more likely to last, grow, and bring fulfillment. Through conscious navigation of trust and doubt, you cultivate connections that are both resilient and meaningful, enhancing your sense of security and well-being across all areas of life.

6: Trusting in Principles Over Personalities

In settings where trust can feel uncertain—due to unreliable behavior, ethical concerns, or high-stakes situations—**principle-based trust** offers a way to build reliable connections grounded in **values, standards, and shared rules** rather than on individuals. Trusting in principles means placing confidence in **ethical frameworks and shared commitments** rather than personalities, creating a stable foundation even when individual actions or motives may be questionable. This approach helps us navigate complex environments with clarity and consistency, focusing on shared values and common goals to guide our actions and interactions.

Principle-Based Trust in Unreliable or Ethically Questionable Environments

In environments where individual motives may be unclear or behavior inconsistent, placing trust solely in personalities can be risky. Relying on **principle-based trust** offers a more stable approach, where trust is rooted in shared values and agreed-upon ethical frameworks rather than in individual actions or promises. By aligning with established principles, you can build a **foundation of trust** that remains steady even when individual behavior fluctuates, creating a sense of stability and predictability.

Why Principles Over Personalities?

People are inherently complex and unpredictable. They may act out of self-interest, change their priorities, or occasionally fail to meet expectations. **Trust based solely on personalities is vulnerable to these fluctuations**, leading to potential disappointment or even betrayal when individuals deviate from what we expect. Principle-based trust, however, provides a more consistent and resilient foundation.

Consistency and Stability: Principles and values offer a guide that is unaffected by personal interests, mood changes, or individual circumstances.

For instance, values like integrity, fairness, and respect serve as enduring standards that do not change, no matter who is involved. In a volatile environment, such as a competitive market or a high-stakes project, trusting in principles creates stability where individual reliability may waver.

A Shared Language and Mutual Respect: When people work together based on shared principles, they create a common ground for interaction, even if personal beliefs, backgrounds, or motivations differ. In a diverse organizational setting, for example, aligning on principles like inclusivity, transparency, and accountability ensures that everyone operates with a shared understanding, fostering mutual respect and smooth collaboration. This alignment is especially valuable when navigating teams with varied cultural or professional perspectives, as it offers a unifying framework that transcends individual personalities.

Ideal for New or Unfamiliar Situations: Principle-based trust is particularly beneficial in situations where you may not have enough information about individuals to determine their trustworthiness. In a new business venture, for example, it's often impractical to assess each partner's character in depth. However, if everyone commits to agreed-upon standards—such as fair treatment, transparency in finances, and ethical decision-making—the partnership can proceed with a foundation of trust based on shared commitments, rather than untested personalities.

By focusing on **principles rather than personalities**, you create a trust structure that is less prone to personal failure, allowing everyone to operate with confidence in shared values and a consistent ethical approach.

Building Trust in Principles

Building principle-based trust involves **establishing and upholding clear standards and ethical guidelines** that everyone agrees to follow. This approach emphasizes transparency, accountability, and ethical practices over individual character traits, providing a framework that reduces the impact of individual inconsistencies.

Setting Specific Standards and Ethical Commitments

Principle-based trust starts with a commitment to clear standards. These might include honesty, fairness, and respect, along with specific guidelines relevant to the context, such as open communication, transparency in decision-making, and mutual accountability. By setting these standards up front, you establish a baseline for behavior that everyone agrees to uphold.

Example: In a business partnership, both parties might commit to transparency by agreeing to share financial updates, disclose conflicts of interest, and conduct regular performance reviews. By establishing these practices as standards, trust becomes an outcome of consistent ethical behavior rather than a reliance on personal integrity.

Implementation: Develop a document that outlines the core values, standards, and practices everyone commits to. For example, in a workplace, this could be a code of conduct or an employee handbook. In personal relationships, a simple conversation about shared values and boundaries can be effective. By putting these standards in place, you make it clear that the relationship relies on these principles.

Upholding Accountability Through Agreed-Upon Rules

Accountability is central to principle-based trust. **Agreed-upon rules** provide a structured way to ensure that everyone abides by the established standards, even when individual motivations may vary. This reduces the risk of breaches in trust because individuals know that there are concrete expectations and methods for addressing lapses.

Example: In an organizational setting, implementing regular check-ins and transparent reporting systems keeps everyone accountable to the agreed principles. If a team member fails to uphold these standards, the focus can shift from personal blame to reinforcing the principle itself. This helps to keep relationships constructive and trust resilient, as accountability is directed toward maintaining the shared values.

Implementation: Establish protocols for addressing breaches of trust. This could include a system for documenting incidents, a process for resolving conflicts based on agreed principles, or a plan for revisiting and reinforcing core values. Knowing there is a clear framework for accountability allows everyone involved to trust the integrity of the process rather than individual intentions alone.

Maintaining Transparency and Open Communication

Transparency is a cornerstone of principle-based trust. When decisions, actions, and information are shared openly, it reduces suspicion and reinforces that everyone is operating under the same ethical guidelines. Open communication allows individuals to address issues as they arise, keeping the relationship or organization aligned with shared principles.

Example: In a family setting, maintaining open communication around finances or household responsibilities can help build trust even if individual family members occasionally make mistakes. By focusing on transparency and ethical guidelines for how family decisions are made, everyone can rely on the integrity of the family's shared principles rather than on individual behavior.

Implementation: Create opportunities for regular communication. This could involve weekly team meetings in a work setting, monthly family discussions, or routine check-ins with friends or partners. These conversations provide a platform to reinforce the principles, address challenges, and celebrate successes, helping everyone feel invested in the shared ethical framework.

Building trust in principles provides a **clear and consistent foundation**, ensuring that trust is directed at values and actions everyone can agree upon rather than at unpredictable individual personalities.

The Strength of Principle-Based Trust in Complex Situations

Principle-based trust offers unique resilience in **complex or ethically ambiguous environments**, where personal reliability may vary. This approach empowers you to maintain integrity and focus on constructive solutions when individuals fall short or when situations become challenging.

Trusting the Process Rather Than Individuals: In principle-based trust, the emphasis is on trusting the process—relying on the standards, rules, and ethical guidelines everyone agreed to uphold. This approach makes it easier to stay aligned even when people make mistakes or when circumstances change. For instance, if a colleague misses a deadline, the focus can remain on revisiting shared values of accountability and transparency rather than on criticizing the individual. This allows for a constructive conversation and preserves trust in the process.

A Resilient Response to Breaches of Trust: When trust is based on principles, breaches of trust are seen as opportunities to reinforce or clarify the values and expectations everyone has agreed upon. If principles are violated, the response involves addressing the issue according to the framework rather than making it personal. For example, if a business partner fails to meet transparency standards, the focus remains on re-establishing that commitment rather than questioning the partner's character. This resilience reduces the emotional toll of breaches, as the shared values provide a clear way to move forward.

Navigating Ethical Ambiguities with Clarity: In situations where ethics may be complex or ambiguous, principle-based trust provides clarity. Rather than making subjective judgments, individuals can refer to agreed-upon standards to guide decisions. In leadership, for example, if a decision has moral implications, leaders can refer to core principles such as fairness and transparency to ensure consistency and integrity in their choice. This clarity minimizes conflict, as everyone understands the basis for decisions.

Principle-based trust acts as a **steady compass** in environments where individual reliability might fluctuate, offering a structure that guides interactions based on shared ethical commitments.

Principle-Based Trust as a Foundation for Reliable and Resilient Relationships

In both professional and personal contexts, principle-based trust is a powerful tool for creating relationships that are **stable, ethical, and resilient**. By aligning on values, ethical standards, and accountability, you establish a structure for trust that is adaptable, clear, and capable of withstanding changes in individual behavior or external challenges.

Ideal for High-Stakes and High-Risk Situations: In high-stakes environments, such as financial ventures or sensitive projects, principle-based trust reduces the impact of individual unpredictability. By focusing on agreed standards, everyone can navigate risks with a shared sense of accountability, improving decision-making and minimizing potential breaches of trust.

Promotes Constructive Accountability: By directing accountability toward maintaining principles, individuals feel a responsibility to uphold values rather than fearing personal criticism. This approach encourages growth, constructive feedback, and a commitment to ethical behavior without compromising personal respect.

Fosters Long-Term Trustworthiness: Principle-based trust builds a lasting foundation that can adapt to different personalities, challenges, and goals. Because it is rooted in shared values, it allows relationships to evolve without becoming dependent on specific people or subjective judgments. This adaptability supports the growth of relationships and partnerships over time.

Principle-based trust **protects integrity and fosters resilience**, providing a clear and reliable way to build trust in any environment—especially in settings where personalities might fluctuate, but principles remain steady. By centering relationships around values rather than individuals, you establish a foundation of trust that can withstand challenges, navigate ambiguities, and create meaningful, enduring connections based on mutual respect and shared ethical commitments.

Aligning Trust with Shared Values, Ethical Standards, and Agreed-Upon Rules

Principle-based trust is founded on the idea that **shared values, ethical standards, and clear rules** create a reliable and resilient foundation for relationships. When trust is aligned with these elements, it becomes less vulnerable to the inconsistencies of individual behavior. By setting explicit guidelines for behavior and accountability, we can foster trust that's grounded in **mutual respect, clear expectations, and ethical alignment**. This approach provides a strong framework for trust in both personal and professional settings, ensuring that everyone involved understands and upholds a common ethical standard.

Defining Core Values and Ethical Standards

Defining core values and ethical standards is the first step in establishing principle-based trust. This involves identifying the fundamental values that should guide the relationship and creating objective ethical standards to anchor behavior, ensuring alignment and respect.

Identify Common Values

Identifying shared values creates a **moral and ethical foundation** that everyone can rely on. These values serve as guiding principles, setting the tone for interactions, decisions, and expectations in the relationship or collaboration.

Professional Setting: In a business or organizational context, common values might include honesty, transparency, accountability, and mutual respect. For example, a team might agree on transparency as a core value, committing to open communication and clear documentation of project milestones. This way, each team member understands the importance of keeping each other informed and respects the transparency needed for collective success.

Personal Relationships: In personal relationships, common values might focus on empathy, support, integrity, and respect. For instance, friends might prioritize empathy by committing to listening without judgment and offering support in times of need. By defining these values explicitly, both individuals understand the expectations and goals of the relationship.

Implementation Tip: Start by discussing values with all parties involved. Reflect on what matters most to each individual, and find values that align. Document these values, and refer to them as a foundation for the relationship, reinforcing them in conversations and actions.

Establish Ethical Standards

Ethical standards provide **objective guidelines for behavior**. In organizations, these may be formalized as codes of conduct, anti-corruption policies, or ethical guidelines for decision-making. In personal or family contexts, ethical standards could reflect commitments to honesty, consistency, and self-respect.

Organizational Examples: Many companies adopt a code of conduct that outlines acceptable behaviors, standards for professional integrity, and practices that promote inclusivity. These standards help align the organization's actions with its values and offer clear consequences for behavior that violates these expectations.

Personal Examples: In personal relationships, ethical standards might include honesty, mutual respect, and commitment to growth. For instance, two friends might agree that honesty is essential and therefore commit to giving each other constructive feedback, even when it's difficult. This standard helps keep the relationship genuine and supportive.

Implementation Tip: Create a formal or informal document outlining the ethical standards agreed upon, depending on the context. For example, an organization might draft an employee handbook, while friends or family members might simply discuss these standards openly. Revisit these ethical standards periodically to reinforce their importance and make adjustments if necessary.

Examples in Action

Business Setting: In a company, an ethical standard like a "commitment to fairness" could mean that all employees and leaders treat each other with respect, provide equal opportunities, and ensure fairness in hiring and promotions. This standard builds trust within the organization by promoting transparency and ethical behavior at every level.

Personal Setting: In a friendship, ethical standards like "respect and honesty" guide both friends to communicate openly, respect each other's boundaries, and offer support when needed. These shared ethical commitments strengthen the friendship by creating a consistent foundation for trust, even when challenges arise.

By defining core values and ethical standards, you create a **clear foundation for trust** that focuses on principles over personalities, ensuring alignment and respect across all interactions.

Implementing Agreed-Upon Rules and Protocols

Agreed-upon rules and protocols provide **structure and accountability** for principle-based trust. They clarify what is expected from each person and offer a framework for maintaining trust, especially in complex or high-stakes settings. These guidelines help manage potential conflicts, define roles, and provide stability to relationships.

Create Clear Rules for Accountability

Agreed-upon rules establish a framework that ensures everyone knows what is expected, how their actions will be measured, and what consequences exist for breaches. These rules are designed to align with shared values and ethical standards, making trust a structured process.

Professional Setting: In a business partnership, rules around transparency—such as regular financial updates or open records—allow each partner to trust the process and the established guidelines, reducing the risk of misunderstandings. For instance, partners might agree on quarterly financial reviews to ensure ongoing transparency.

Personal Setting: In a family or relationship, accountability rules might include openly discussing responsibilities or checking in on mutual goals. For example, partners might agree to set weekly check-ins to discuss finances, household responsibilities, or personal goals. These rules ensure that both partners feel supported and that trust is actively maintained.

Implementation Tip: Document the rules in an accessible way, such as a contract, agreement, or shared note. Ensure that everyone understands their role and the specific expectations. Regularly revisit and update these rules to accommodate evolving goals or challenges.

Establish Guidelines for Conflict Resolution

A conflict resolution protocol keeps **disagreements constructive** and prevents personal biases from eroding trust. Having clear, predefined steps for handling conflicts ensures that any issues are addressed in line with agreed-upon principles, reducing emotional fallout and misunderstandings.

Professional Setting: In a leadership team, a conflict resolution protocol might involve discussing issues openly in team meetings, addressing misunderstandings directly, or consulting a third-party mediator if needed. This approach reinforces that conflicts are not personal but are simply part of the process, encouraging respect and fairness.

Personal Setting: In a family setting, conflict resolution guidelines might include giving each person an equal opportunity to express their perspective, practicing active listening, or taking a "cooling-off" period if emotions run high. These steps help prevent conflicts from escalating and maintain trust by keeping disagreements focused on issues rather than personal attacks.

Implementation Tip: Write down the conflict resolution steps and discuss them with everyone involved. Agree on the steps ahead of time to avoid misunderstandings when tensions arise. Refer back to these steps whenever conflicts occur, reinforcing a constructive, principle-based approach to problem-solving.

Examples in Action

Team Project: In a project team, agreed-upon rules might include accountability measures like weekly progress reports, transparency in communication, and clearly defined roles. These rules ensure that each team member knows their responsibilities and feels valued, creating a sense of collective trust.

Family Setting: In a family, rules around shared responsibilities, open discussions, and respect for each person's time create a framework where each family member feels seen and appreciated. For example, parents might establish routines where everyone contributes to household chores or shares weekly updates on family schedules.

Rules and protocols add **structure and stability** to principle-based trust, allowing everyone to trust the integrity of the process, even when interpersonal relationships fluctuate.

The Value of Principle-Based Trust Through Values, Standards, and Rules

Aligning trust with shared values, ethical standards, and agreed-upon rules provides a **resilient framework** for building and maintaining trust across various contexts. This alignment allows you to focus on the integrity of the process and shared ethical commitments, rather than relying solely on individual personalities, which can be unpredictable.

Consistency Across Contexts: Principle-based trust provides a foundation that is applicable in both personal and professional settings, allowing individuals to navigate relationships with integrity and consistency. Whether in a friendship, a family, or a corporate team, shared values and standards create a cohesive basis for trust that can withstand challenges.

Reducing Emotional Vulnerability: By emphasizing principles over personalities, principle-based trust reduces the emotional vulnerabilities that come with relying heavily on individual actions or intentions. Knowing that everyone involved is held to the same standards and rules makes it easier to manage disappointments or breaches of trust.

Building Long-Term Resilience: Principle-based trust cultivates a form of trust that is more resilient to the inevitable ups and downs of life. Because trust is rooted in values and protocols, it remains intact even when people make mistakes or encounter challenges, allowing relationships to grow and adapt over time.

In conclusion, **aligning trust with shared values, ethical standards, and agreed-upon rules** creates a solid foundation for reliable, resilient relationships. This approach fosters accountability, promotes fairness, and reduces misunderstandings, making it easier to trust in the process and ethical commitments that have been collectively defined. Principle-based trust ensures that connections are built on integrity and respect, creating relationships that are not only trustworthy but also adaptable to change and complexity.

Examples of Principle-Based Trust in Business, Leadership, and Personal Growth

Principle-based trust is versatile and can be applied across different areas, from professional environments to personal development. It relies on **shared values, ethical standards, and consistent practices** to build trust that goes beyond individual personalities. By anchoring trust in principles, we create relationships and environments that are **fair, transparent, and resilient**. Let's explore specific examples of how principle-based trust can be implemented in business, leadership, and personal growth, along with practical strategies for doing so.

Principle-Based Trust in Business

In business, principle-based trust focuses on **shared ethical commitments** that guide interactions, decisions, and partnerships. Rather than placing trust solely in individuals, organizations and partners can rely on transparent policies, ethical codes, and formal agreements to build a **predictable and fair business environment**. This approach minimizes reliance on personal character and promotes consistent, ethical behavior across the board.

Example: Ethical Standards in Business Partnerships

In a business partnership, two companies might agree to specific ethical standards, such as fair pricing, clear communication, and transparent accounting practices. Rather than depending on individual relationships, the partnership is grounded in shared principles, ensuring that both parties align on fundamental expectations. If disagreements arise, they can reference these shared standards, providing an objective foundation for addressing issues fairly.

Scenario: Two tech companies form a strategic alliance to develop new software. They agree on principles of fairness and transparency, setting up rules around revenue-sharing, intellectual property rights, and responsibilities. If a dispute arises over intellectual property, they rely on their previously agreed-upon standards rather than personal biases to find a resolution. This objective approach strengthens the partnership by building trust in the ethical framework.

Implementation Tip: Develop a Code of Ethics or Memorandum of Understanding (MOU)

A **code of ethics** or an **MOU** can outline the values, expectations, and protocols for handling conflicts in a business partnership. This document serves as a reference point for both parties, ensuring that decisions are aligned with the shared principles.

Practical Steps:

Identify and agree upon core values with all involved parties, such as fairness, transparency, and accountability.

Draft a clear, written agreement that includes guidelines for ethical behavior, communication protocols, and conflict-resolution methods.

Make the code of ethics easily accessible and revisit it regularly to ensure alignment with evolving goals or challenges in the partnership.

A well-drafted MOU or code of ethics creates **clarity, aligns actions with principles**, and provides a solid framework for accountability, promoting sustainable trust in business.

Principle-Based Trust in Leadership

In leadership, principle-based trust is about creating a **culture of accountability, transparency, and fairness** that supports ethical decision-making and builds trust across the organization. Leaders who emphasize principles over personalities foster an environment where trust is rooted in **consistent practices** rather than individual loyalty or favoritism. This approach empowers teams to rely on **systemic integrity** rather than subjective judgment.

Example: Transparent and Fair Leadership Practices

A leader who prioritizes transparency and fairness may implement policies for open communication, such as holding regular team meetings where each team member has the opportunity to voice ideas and concerns. By consistently upholding these practices, the leader builds trust based on predictability and ethical action rather than on personal style. Employees come to trust the leader not because of their charisma but because of their **commitment to principles** that promote inclusivity and fairness.

Scenario: In a large organization, a department head commits to transparent decision-making by involving team members in goal-setting processes and sharing progress openly. When team members express concerns about resource allocation, the leader addresses the issue in a team meeting, explaining the rationale behind decisions and inviting feedback. This open approach establishes trust in the leader's fairness and reinforces the department's commitment to collaboration.

Implementation Tip: Establish Transparent Policies for Decision-Making, Communication, and Rewards

Transparent policies ensure that all employees have **equal access to information** and understand the basis for decisions and rewards. This creates a culture where trust is directed toward the ethical standards of the organization rather than toward individual leaders alone.

Practical Steps:

Develop policies that clarify the decision-making process, making it transparent and inclusive.

Hold regular team meetings to communicate updates, set goals, and address concerns, reinforcing the values of fairness and inclusivity.

Create a rewards system based on objective performance metrics rather than subjective assessments, ensuring employees see the organization as committed to equality.

By promoting transparency, open communication, and fairness, leaders can cultivate **organization-wide trust** that extends beyond individual relationships, creating a work environment where people feel valued and respected.

Principle-Based Trust in Personal Growth

Principle-based trust isn't just for professional settings; it's also an essential tool for **personal growth**. When individuals align their actions with their core values, they build a trustworthy relationship with themselves, which fosters confidence, resilience, and self-respect. Principle-based trust in personal growth means making choices that reflect one's own principles and living with **integrity**.

Example: Self-Reflection and Ethical Alignment in Personal Growth

If a person values authenticity and self-respect, they might commit to self-reflection, seek honest feedback, and avoid situations that compromise their values. By consistently acting in alignment with these principles, they cultivate a **trustworthy relationship with themselves**. This self-trust enables them to make confident decisions, knowing they are acting in harmony with their values.

Scenario: An individual striving for authenticity sets aside time each week for self-reflection, assessing whether their recent actions align with their core values. When faced with a career opportunity that conflicts with their personal principles, they respectfully decline, trusting that staying true to their values will lead them to opportunities that better align with their ethics. This ongoing alignment reinforces their self-trust and encourages further growth.

Implementation Tip: Develop a Personal Code of Ethics or List of Guiding Principles

A personal code of ethics is a powerful tool for aligning actions with values, helping individuals create a foundation of **self-trust and integrity**. This list of principles serves as a compass, guiding personal decisions and actions.

Practical Steps:

Identify your core values—those that you are unwilling to compromise, such as honesty, self-respect, or compassion.

Write down these values as a personal code of ethics, and refer to them when making decisions or evaluating behavior.

Set aside regular check-in times for reflection, using your code of ethics to assess whether your actions align with your principles.

A personal code of ethics fosters self-trust and encourages growth based on **authentic alignment** with one's values, empowering individuals to make resilient, value-driven choices.

The Broader Impact of Principle-Based Trust Across Contexts

Whether in business, leadership, or personal development, principle-based trust creates relationships and environments that are **rooted in shared values, ethical standards, and clear expectations**. By anchoring trust in principles, we make it resilient to the fluctuations of individual behavior and more adaptable to challenges and growth.

Sustainability Across Relationships: Principle-based trust creates a foundation that remains stable across different relationships and situations. In a business context, this ensures that partnerships are reliable; in leadership, it promotes a fair, transparent culture; and in personal growth, it provides a roadmap for authentic decision-making.

Clarity and Accountability: By relying on shared principles, everyone involved understands the expectations and is held to the same standards. This clarity reduces misunderstandings and promotes accountability, building trust that is both measurable and meaningful.

Empowerment and Resilience: When trust is based on principles, individuals and teams feel empowered to make decisions aligned with these values. This strengthens resilience, as decisions and actions are grounded in ethical standards that provide consistency even in challenging situations.

In summary, principle-based trust is a powerful, versatile approach that supports **sustainable, value-driven relationships**. By aligning with shared values, ethical standards, and agreed-upon rules, you create a trust framework that encourages clarity, integrity, and accountability across all areas of life. This approach to trust is not only adaptable but also fosters an environment where people can thrive—knowing they are part of relationships and organizations that value principles over personalities.

How to Implement Principle-Based Trust

Implementing principle-based trust requires **consistency in values, transparency in actions, and accountability** to ensure that trust is anchored in integrity. Principle-based trust allows us to build resilient relationships, whether in personal, professional, or organizational contexts. Here's a guide for integrating principle-based trust into your relationships and environments.

Define Your Core Principles

Start by identifying and defining the values and ethical standards that will serve as the **foundation of the relationship or project**. These core principles act as a moral compass, providing direction and consistency across interactions.

Reflect on Core Values: Think about what matters most in this specific context. For example, in a work project, values might include transparency, fairness, and respect for deadlines. In a personal relationship, they might center around honesty, empathy, and mutual respect. Choosing values that align with the purpose and goals of the relationship creates a strong basis for principle-based trust.

Gain Consensus: In collaborative settings, discuss these principles with all involved parties to ensure alignment. It's essential that everyone agrees on these values, as they will form the backbone of the trust framework. Achieving consensus empowers each person to feel accountable to the shared values.

Practical Tip: Make a list of the chosen values and display them as a reference point, whether on a shared platform, in a workspace, or as part of a written agreement. This visible reminder keeps the focus on principles.

Set Clear Expectations

Setting clear expectations involves defining the **rules, boundaries, and behaviors** that will uphold the principles. Clarity in expectations reduces ambiguity and creates a structured approach to trust that focuses on principles rather than individuals.

Establish Standards for Behavior and Communication: Outline what behavior and communication styles align with the chosen values. In a work setting, this might mean maintaining professionalism in all communications and meeting deadlines reliably. In personal relationships, it could mean prioritizing respectful dialogue during disagreements.

Define Boundaries and Accountability: Discuss what actions or behaviors could potentially breach trust and clarify the boundaries for each relationship. Setting boundaries early helps people understand the limits and ensures they're aware of the standards they're accountable to.

Practical Tip: Create a document outlining these expectations, and review it together to ensure everyone is on the same page. Encourage questions or clarifications to promote transparency and avoid misunderstandings. For instance, if timeliness is a core value, specify expectations around meeting deadlines and reporting delays.

Document Agreements and Protocols

Formalizing the principles, standards, and expectations in writing adds structure and provides a consistent point of reference. This documentation can take the form of an **agreement, code of conduct, or set of protocols**, which reinforces trust by aligning everyone with shared standards.

Create a Written Agreement or Code of Conduct: This document should summarize the agreed-upon values, standards, expectations, and rules of engagement. Having these in writing makes it easier to reference them later, especially if issues arise.

Include Conflict-Resolution Protocols: Outline procedures for handling disagreements or misunderstandings in a constructive way. When principles are violated, the focus should be on addressing the issue within the framework of the agreed-upon standards rather than resorting to blame.

Practical Tip: Make the document easily accessible to everyone involved, such as via a shared drive or in a physical space. For more formal settings, consider asking all parties to sign it, signaling commitment to these principles. In personal relationships, this document might be more informal but could still include key points that both parties can refer back to.

Practice Regular Check-Ins and Open Communication

Principle-based trust thrives on **consistent reinforcement and open dialogue**. Regular check-ins help ensure alignment with principles, provide space for feedback, and keep communication channels open for addressing any challenges.

Schedule Regular Check-Ins: These meetings or conversations should be structured to review how well each party is upholding the principles and to discuss any adjustments needed. In professional settings, weekly or monthly check-ins can keep everyone accountable. In personal relationships, periodic conversations can serve as gentle reminders of mutual commitments.

Foster a Safe Space for Feedback: Encourage honest feedback about how well everyone is aligning with the principles. This open communication reinforces trust, as individuals feel valued and respected when their perspectives are acknowledged.

Practical Tip: Use a structured agenda for check-ins to ensure that the discussion stays focused on the principles and expectations. You might ask each participant to share one area where they feel aligned and one where they'd like to improve, creating a collaborative environment for growth.

Review and Reassess as Needed

Relationships and projects evolve over time, so it's important to periodically **review and reassess** the principles, expectations, and standards guiding the relationship. Adapting principles as necessary helps to maintain relevance and alignment with the current dynamics, keeping trust rooted in real, evolving needs.

Periodically Evaluate the Principles and Standards: Assess whether the initial principles and rules still serve the relationship's needs or if adjustments are needed. For instance, if the project scope changes, the values around flexibility and adaptability may need to be emphasized.

Allow Room for Adjustment: Life and work are dynamic, and principles that served well at the start may need revisiting as relationships deepen or challenges arise. For example, a team working on a tight deadline might need to shift emphasis from thoroughness to efficiency, temporarily adjusting expectations around review processes.

Practical Tip: Schedule an annual or biannual review of principles in professional settings, or check in at natural transition points in personal relationships. This can include refreshing documentation, discussing changes in roles, and evaluating adherence to the values that sustain trust.

Building Resilient Relationships Through Principle-Based Trust

By implementing principle-based trust, you build relationships that are **resilient, clear, and consistent**, creating a reliable foundation that can withstand challenges and uncertainties. This approach helps reduce ambiguity, reinforces mutual respect, and supports trust that's deeply grounded in shared ethical commitments.

Promotes Accountability and Integrity: With clear principles and expectations, everyone knows they're accountable to a common standard, fostering an environment where accountability is shared and trust is maintained without dependence on individual personalities.

Encourages Constructive Growth: Principle-based trust allows room for growth and adaptation without compromising on core values. When individuals or teams know they are held to high standards, they are motivated to engage with integrity and collaborate openly, strengthening both individual and group resilience.

Provides a Stable Foundation in Changing Dynamics: When relationships are built on principles rather than individuals, they are better equipped to navigate change. Trust remains steady, as it's based on shared ethics and agreed-upon practices rather than fluctuating with personal changes.

By focusing on **shared values and ethical commitments**, principle-based trust fosters relationships that are not only stable but also adaptable and empowering. This approach allows individuals and teams to trust each other in a way that's clear, consistent, and deeply grounded in integrity, creating environments of mutual respect and accountability that can evolve as needed.

7: Emotional Resilience—Protecting Yourself While Trusting Others

In a world where trust can often be tested, **emotional resilience** is crucial. It allows us to manage trust with a balanced perspective, even when doubt or ethical uncertainties arise. Building emotional resilience helps us remain open to connection while protecting our inner well-being, providing a buffer against disappointments and reinforcing our capacity to trust with wisdom. This chapter explores how to cultivate emotional resilience in relationships, offering practices to maintain balance, strategies for boundary-setting, and approaches for recovering from trust breaches without becoming overly cynical.

The Role of Emotional Resilience in Managing Trust with Doubt

Emotional resilience plays a crucial role in **balancing trust with doubt** and helps us engage in relationships with wisdom and self-protection. It supports our ability to navigate complex interactions, enabling us to remain grounded even when trust is tested by ethical dilemmas, changing intentions, or misunderstandings. Emotional resilience helps us maintain a **healthy, flexible trust** that can withstand challenges, allowing us to engage with others without compromising our well-being.

Protecting Inner Well-Being

Emotional resilience creates an **internal foundation** that enables us to handle trust-related challenges calmly and constructively. By developing resilience, we are better equipped to manage the fluctuations in trust that naturally occur in relationships, helping us to avoid emotional volatility when trust is put to the test.

Staying Calm Amid Doubt: When trust is challenged—perhaps due to a colleague's questionable actions or a friend's unexpected behavior—resilience allows us to pause, assess the situation thoughtfully, and respond mindfully. Rather than reacting impulsively or immediately assuming the worst, we stay grounded, maintaining an internal steadiness that enables clear thinking.

Reducing Reactivity: Emotional resilience helps prevent us from letting moments of doubt or uncertainty disrupt our sense of stability. For example, if someone makes a disappointing choice, resilience enables us to take a step back and assess whether it is a minor misstep or part of a larger pattern. This reflective approach allows us to respond without letting emotions take over, reducing unnecessary drama or misunderstandings.

Empowering Thoughtful Responses: By grounding ourselves internally, we gain the capacity to choose our responses carefully. Rather than letting doubt or disappointment drive our actions, we can make decisions based on our values and boundaries, upholding our inner well-being even in challenging situations.

Emotional resilience acts as a **protective shield** for our inner well-being, allowing us to engage in relationships without feeling overly exposed or reactive to every shift in trust.

Balancing Trust with Realism

Emotional resilience also helps us strike a **balance between openness and caution**, ensuring that we remain engaged in relationships without overextending ourselves. This balance allows us to trust thoughtfully, considering both the potential and the risks of trust, which helps us stay optimistic without disregarding reality.

Practicing Cautious Optimism: Resilience supports a form of trust that is open yet aware of the complexities of human behavior. Instead of assuming that everyone is fully trustworthy, resilience gives us a steady perspective, allowing us to trust with both hope and discernment. For instance, if we're working with a new colleague, emotional resilience helps us stay optimistic about the partnership while remaining mindful of signs that may require setting boundaries.

Acknowledging Potential Risks: Trusting with emotional resilience means recognizing that trust is rarely black-and-white. While we may believe in the goodness of others, resilience helps us remain alert to potential red flags without becoming overly suspicious. This balanced approach helps us protect ourselves without becoming overly guarded, allowing trust to develop naturally.

Avoiding Over-Vulnerability: Emotional resilience ensures that we don't overextend our trust to the point of feeling vulnerable. When trust is balanced with realism, we can avoid placing too much of ourselves into relationships prematurely. For example, in a new friendship, resilience allows us to share parts of ourselves while holding back until mutual trust is established, giving the relationship time to grow.

By balancing trust with realism, emotional resilience fosters a **measured approach to trust**, where we can engage meaningfully without losing our footing.

Adapting to Disappointments

Emotional resilience prepares us to handle **disappointments gracefully** without internalizing them as personal failures. When trust is breached, resilient individuals are able to reflect on the experience, extract valuable insights, and move forward with a strengthened perspective. Rather than becoming cynical or bitter, they learn to **adapt and recover**, maintaining their faith in the importance of trust.

Viewing Disappointments as Opportunities for Growth: Emotional resilience helps us see trust breaches not as losses but as learning experiences. When trust is broken, resilience allows us to step back, examine what went wrong, and use the experience as a foundation for wiser trust in the future. For example, if a friend repeatedly breaks promises, resilience enables us to recognize this pattern and adjust our expectations, rather than feeling discouraged or hurt.

Maintaining Faith in Our Values: Rather than letting disappointment shake our core beliefs, resilience allows us to hold onto our values. We may adjust our expectations, but we don't lose faith in the principles we stand by. For instance, if someone takes advantage of our trust, we might adjust our boundaries with that individual while still valuing honesty and integrity in other relationships.

Avoiding Cynicism and Bitterness: Emotionally resilient individuals can recover from trust breaches without letting one experience tarnish their perspective on all relationships. Resilience protects against the urge to become overly guarded, enabling us to maintain an open heart while being more discerning. This approach prevents us from falling into cynicism and keeps us receptive to genuine connections.

Emotional resilience empowers us to **transform disappointments into growth opportunities**, allowing us to adapt and evolve rather than becoming overly protective or closed off.

Emotional Resilience as an Anchor for Trust

In sum, emotional resilience serves as an **emotional anchor**, helping us sustain healthy, adaptable trust even in ethically ambiguous situations. By protecting our inner well-being, balancing trust with realism, and adapting to disappointments, we build a resilient trust that is both strong and flexible.

Empowers Intentional Trust Decisions: Emotional resilience gives us the clarity to decide when to extend trust and when to hold back, making trust an intentional choice rather than a reaction. This empowerment ensures that trust aligns with our values and boundaries, fostering a balanced approach that enriches relationships.

Supports Self-Respect and Dignity: Resilience in trust relationships allows us to uphold our dignity, especially when others fall short of our expectations. By focusing on our values and maintaining emotional balance, we engage in relationships with self-respect, honoring our worth without depending solely on external validation.

Enhances Adaptability to Ethical Challenges: Emotional resilience keeps us steady in environments where integrity may be inconsistent. In such contexts, resilience enables us to navigate relationships with caution, adapt to changes, and hold fast to our principles without becoming overly discouraged.

In building emotional resilience, we lay the groundwork for **healthy, adaptable trust** that can withstand life's inevitable ups and downs. We become better equipped to trust in ways that are meaningful and sustainable, able to engage fully without losing our balance. Emotional resilience not only fortifies our sense of self but also strengthens our capacity to form connections that are rooted in respect, wisdom, and inner strength.

Practices for Maintaining Emotional Balance

Maintaining emotional balance is crucial for approaching relationships with a **clear sense of self-protection and clarity**. Emotional balance allows us to engage in trust meaningfully, ensuring our decisions are grounded, intentional, and aligned with our values. By incorporating **mindfulness, boundary-setting, and reflective exercises**, we can fortify our emotional resilience, making it easier to navigate trust with both confidence and caution.

Mindfulness Practices

Mindfulness helps us develop **present-moment awareness**, which enables us to observe emotions, thoughts, and reactions without judgment. This clarity helps us make trust-related decisions with composure, especially when doubt or uncertainty arises.

Pause and Reflect

When faced with a trust-related decision, taking a moment to pause can prevent impulsive reactions driven by strong emotions like excitement, caution, or skepticism. This pause gives us space to process emotions and make a **more measured response**.

Example: Suppose a friend shares sensitive information with you, sparking both excitement about the closeness of the friendship and caution about what to share in return. By pausing to reflect, you allow yourself to engage mindfully, responding with consideration for both the relationship and your boundaries.

Focus on Breath Awareness

Deep breathing techniques can help center our emotions, especially in high-stakes or challenging situations where emotions may run high. Focusing on breathing activates the **body's relaxation response**, helping us manage stress and regain composure.

Example: When you're disappointed by someone's actions—such as a colleague missing a deadline—taking a few moments to breathe deeply helps you release immediate frustration. This allows you to approach the situation with patience and avoid reactive responses.

Practical Tip

Dedicate a few minutes daily to mindfulness meditation, where you simply observe thoughts and emotions as they arise without trying to control or suppress them. This practice gradually builds emotional resilience, creating a buffer against the impact of unexpected trust breaches or disappointments.

Setting Boundaries

Boundaries are **protective guidelines** that enable us to engage in relationships with self-respect and prevent overextension. They help manage expectations by defining limits, ensuring that we maintain a balance between trust and self-protection.

Define Your Limits

Clarifying your boundaries means understanding where you feel comfortable extending trust and where you prefer to hold back. For instance, you may be open to sharing personal stories with friends but choose to keep financial matters private. By defining these limits, you create a structure that allows trust to grow **within safe, clear parameters.**

Example: If you feel comfortable trusting a new friend with general life updates but want to avoid sharing work-related stress, defining this boundary helps you enjoy the friendship without feeling overexposed.

Communicate Boundaries Clearly

Clearly and calmly communicating your boundaries helps maintain balance in relationships and reinforces mutual respect. By expressing what you're comfortable with, you establish a foundation where both parties understand and honor each other's limits.

Example: In a professional setting, you might tell a colleague, "I'm comfortable collaborating on projects, but I prefer to keep my personal life separate from work discussions." This open communication ensures that both of you have clear expectations, promoting a balanced and respectful work relationship.

Practical Tip

Write down your boundaries, specifying areas where you feel comfortable extending trust and where you prefer to exercise caution. Revisit these boundaries regularly, especially if circumstances or relationships evolve. Regular reassessment ensures that your boundaries stay **aligned with your values and current needs**.

Reflective Exercises

Reflective exercises allow us to **explore and understand our trust patterns** and emotional triggers. By engaging in reflection, we gain clarity on past experiences, helping us approach future trust situations with increased awareness and adaptability.

Journaling

Journaling about trust experiences provides a space to explore emotions, challenges, and patterns in relationships. Writing down your thoughts helps you identify recurring themes, such as situations where trust was tested, areas where you felt vulnerable, or moments of disappointment. This self-awareness enables you to adjust your approach to trust when necessary.

Example: If you journal about a friendship where trust was broken, you may notice patterns in the friend's behavior that you initially overlooked. This insight helps you approach future friendships with a better understanding of the red flags to watch for.

Learning from Past Experiences

Reflecting on past trust breaches or disappointments provides valuable insights for future interactions. Consider what you learned from each experience, whether there were any warning signs, or if there were emotional reactions or expectations that need adjusting.

Example: After a business partnership fails due to a lack of transparency, reflecting on the experience may reveal areas where you could set clearer expectations or verification practices in future partnerships.

Practical Tip

Set aside time each week for journaling or self-reflection, noting recent trust experiences, how they felt, and any lessons learned. By regularly reflecting on these experiences, you cultivate a mindset of growth, learning to adapt and strengthen your resilience over time.

The Benefits of Practicing Emotional Balance

Integrating mindfulness, boundaries, and reflection into your life supports emotional balance and enables you to engage in relationships with **thoughtfulness, protection, and empowerment**. These practices provide a structure that strengthens inner resilience, allowing you to manage trust with clarity and confidence.

Increased Self-Awareness: Regular mindfulness and reflection help you stay aware of your emotions, needs, and boundaries. This heightened self-awareness enables you to approach trust thoughtfully, ensuring it aligns with your comfort level.

Greater Resilience to Disappointment: Emotional balance supports your ability to recover from trust breaches without internalizing them or becoming overly guarded. When trust is broken, resilience enables you to process the experience, learn from it, and move forward without losing faith in trust altogether.

Healthier Relationships: By setting boundaries and practicing mindfulness, you create relationships where trust grows within a safe, respectful framework. This approach allows connections to thrive without compromising your sense of self-protection or well-being.

Through these practices, you can build **emotionally balanced relationships** that are grounded in respect, trust, and integrity. Emotional balance enables you to engage fully without feeling exposed, fostering relationships where trust is both meaningful and sustainable.

Strategies for Recovering from Trust Breaches Without Cynicism

Recovering from a breach of trust can be emotionally demanding, but resilience allows us to **heal without becoming cynical or overly guarded**. By processing emotions, learning from the experience, and practicing forgiveness, we can approach future relationships with a cautious yet positive outlook. The goal is to integrate the lessons from trust breaches, empowering us to trust again with wisdom and self-protection.

Process and Accept Your Emotions

The first step in healing from a trust breach is to **acknowledge and accept the emotions** that arise. Suppressing feelings like disappointment, anger, or hurt can lead to resentment, making it harder to trust others in the future. Allowing yourself to experience these emotions openly can provide relief and clarity.

Acknowledge Emotional Reactions

It's natural to feel a range of emotions when trust is broken. Rather than pushing them away, give yourself permission to fully experience them. This may include journaling, talking to a friend, or practicing mindfulness. By exploring these feelings, you can prevent them from taking control of your actions and begin to process them constructively.

Example: Suppose a close friend shares something you confided in them with others. You may feel a mix of betrayal and anger. Taking time to journal about your feelings allows you to acknowledge these reactions without judgment, creating space to process the experience.

Avoid Self-Blame

Trust breaches often reflect the other person's choices rather than your own mistakes. Resist the urge to blame yourself or feel that you should have "seen it coming." Instead, view the breach as a reminder that trust is an evolving process that occasionally requires adjustment.

Example: If a business partner fails to uphold an agreement, avoid questioning your decision-making abilities. Remind yourself that trust inherently involves some risk and that a breach is more about their actions than any fault on your part.

Accepting emotions without judgment creates **emotional release** and clarity, allowing you to move forward without internalizing the experience as a personal failure.

Reframe the Experience as a Learning Opportunity

Viewing a trust breach as a lesson rather than a failure helps turn the experience into a **source of insight**. Each instance of broken trust offers valuable information about human behavior, allowing us to refine how we approach trust and set boundaries.

Identify the Lesson

Reflect on what the breach has taught you about trust dynamics. Perhaps it highlighted areas where stronger boundaries could have been set, or it revealed subtle red flags that may have gone unnoticed. By identifying these lessons, you gain clarity on how to approach future trust situations with a more discerning mindset.

Example: If a colleague repeatedly overpromises and underdelivers, the lesson might be to set clear expectations early on in future partnerships. Reflecting on this pattern enables you to notice similar signs with others, helping you make wiser trust decisions.

Adapt Your Boundaries and Expectations

Use what you've learned to fine-tune your approach to setting boundaries or managing expectations in future relationships. This doesn't mean becoming guarded; it means being intentional and aware. Adjusting your trust approach based on lessons learned encourages a **healthy balance between openness and self-protection**.

Example: After a friend fails to respect a boundary you set, you might adapt by communicating boundaries more assertively in future friendships. This adaptation allows you to remain open to connection while protecting your well-being.

Reframing trust breaches as learning opportunities helps you gain **constructive insight** rather than seeing the experience as a setback, empowering you to trust again with renewed clarity and confidence.

Practice Forgiveness and Release

Forgiveness is a powerful tool for healing, helping us let go of the emotional weight of a trust breach and move forward with clarity. Holding onto resentment can create emotional barriers to new relationships, while forgiveness opens the door to future connections. Whether it involves forgiving the other person or yourself, **practicing forgiveness promotes inner peace and resilience**.

Forgive the Other Person

Forgiveness doesn't mean excusing their actions; rather, it's about releasing the emotional hold their behavior has on you. Recognize that the trust breach is a reflection of their choices, which you can't control, and that dwelling on it only prolongs your pain. Letting go frees you from the past and helps you focus on healthier relationships.

Example: If a friend fails to show up during a difficult time, forgiving them allows you to release bitterness and see the friendship for what it is, rather than dwelling on disappointment. This frees up emotional space to appreciate connections with those who have been supportive.

Forgive Yourself

After a trust breach, it's common to feel regret about having trusted in the first place. Practicing self-forgiveness helps you move forward without internalizing the experience as a personal failing. Remind yourself that trusting others is an act of courage and that learning from experiences is part of growth.

Example: If you trusted a coworker who later took credit for your work, avoid punishing yourself for the misplaced trust. Forgiving yourself allows you to accept the experience as a learning opportunity without becoming overly cautious or mistrusting in the future.

Practical Tip: Write a Forgiveness Letter

Writing a letter expressing forgiveness—whether you intend to send it or not—can be a powerful release. Acknowledge the impact of the trust breach, articulate how it affected you, and affirm your commitment to growth and resilience. This practice can help **release lingering emotions** and support a positive outlook.

Example: In your letter, you might write to the person who broke your trust, explaining the hurt they caused, but also expressing your intention to move forward without holding onto resentment. This process often brings closure, allowing you to fully release the emotional burden.

Moving Forward with Trust that is Cautious Yet Positive

By processing emotions, reframing trust breaches as lessons, and practicing forgiveness, you can recover from trust challenges without hardening your outlook. These strategies support a **balanced, resilient approach** to trust, where you remain open to new connections without being overly vulnerable.

Encourages Growth and Self-Awareness: Each trust breach can deepen your self-awareness and help you refine your approach to relationships. Instead of viewing it as a setback, you see it as an opportunity to grow and set stronger boundaries.

Promotes Emotional Freedom: Letting go of resentment and forgiving yourself and others prevents past breaches from controlling your emotions and future decisions. This freedom allows you to engage in relationships without carrying emotional baggage.

Fosters Healthier, More Intentional Trust: Trust that is built on learning and resilience becomes intentional and well-considered. It allows you to connect genuinely, knowing that your trust decisions are informed by experience, wisdom, and self-protection.

By integrating these strategies, you cultivate a trust that is both **cautious and positive**, adaptable and open to future relationships. This approach empowers you to recover from breaches gracefully and to re-enter connections with an optimistic, yet grounded, mindset.

Building Resilient, Balanced Trust in Relationships

Emotional resilience is essential for **building trust that is balanced, thoughtful, and sustainable**. Resilient trust allows us to engage in relationships with openness and warmth while maintaining a strong inner foundation, ensuring that we don't become overly vulnerable or compromised. By cultivating resilience, we build relationships where trust is grounded in self-awareness, adaptability, and a commitment to growth. This approach enables us to trust others without sacrificing our well-being.

Enhances Self-Awareness

Emotional resilience encourages a **reflective mindset** that helps us understand our needs, boundaries, and responses in trust situations. This self-awareness is key to developing trust thoughtfully, allowing us to approach relationships with clarity and to adjust our trust based on each relationship's dynamics.

Understanding Personal Boundaries: Resilience helps us recognize and respect our own boundaries, allowing us to set clear limits around trust. This clarity prevents us from overextending ourselves and ensures that we engage with others in a way that honors our needs. For instance, we might trust a friend with personal information but feel comfortable setting boundaries around topics that make us uncomfortable.

Identifying Emotional Triggers: Self-awareness through resilience also helps us recognize our emotional triggers in trust situations. This understanding allows us to manage responses constructively, rather than reacting impulsively. If, for example, we feel uneasy sharing certain information due to past experiences, resilience gives us the presence of mind to navigate that hesitation thoughtfully.

Practical Application: Regular reflection or journaling can help us maintain this self-awareness, providing insight into the areas where we feel comfortable extending trust and where we might need to hold back. Checking in with ourselves on our boundaries and comfort levels in different relationships allows us to engage in trust with clarity and purpose.

By enhancing self-awareness, resilience allows us to **trust thoughtfully**, creating a foundation for balanced, fulfilling connections.

Encourages Growth-Oriented Trust

Emotional resilience supports a **growth-oriented approach to trust** that moves beyond viewing trust as an all-or-nothing decision. Instead, resilience encourages us to see each trust experience as an opportunity for learning and growth, building confidence in our ability to manage trust with skill and intentionality.

Viewing Trust as a Journey: Resilient trust is not static; it evolves as relationships deepen and as we gain new insights. This growth-oriented view allows us to adjust our level of trust gradually, rather than assuming we must fully trust or distrust someone from the start. For instance, in a new professional relationship, we might start with small tasks to build trust, gradually increasing responsibilities as reliability is demonstrated.

Learning from Experience: Resilience helps us process trust breaches as learning opportunities rather than personal failures. This perspective allows us to refine our approach, recognize patterns, and become more discerning in future relationships. Each experience with trust—positive or challenging—adds to our understanding and helps us make wiser trust decisions in the future.

Practical Application: Embracing a growth-oriented approach to trust means reflecting on past trust experiences, both positive and negative, and identifying the lessons they offer. This can include recognizing traits that inspire trust, signs of reliability, or red flags to watch for. By integrating these lessons, we develop a more nuanced and confident approach to trusting others.

A growth-oriented view of trust fosters **continuous learning and adaptability**, empowering us to build connections that are both meaningful and resilient.

Strengthens Adaptability

When trust is grounded in resilience, we become **adaptable in our relationships**, able to respond constructively to trust breaches or shifts in dynamics without losing confidence in our values. Emotional resilience provides a steady anchor that keeps us rooted, allowing trust to remain flexible and dynamic.

Responding to Trust Breaches with Composure: Resilience helps us stay calm and collected when trust is tested or broken, avoiding the emotional extremes of betrayal or withdrawal. This adaptability allows us to address issues constructively, whether that means setting new boundaries, renegotiating expectations, or taking time to reassess the relationship.

Adjusting to Changing Circumstances: As relationships evolve, resilience enables us to adjust our trust level accordingly. For example, a friendship that once felt completely secure might require some new boundaries if the friend goes through a difficult phase that affects their behavior. Resilience allows us to adapt our trust without feeling pressured to maintain it at the same level indefinitely.

Maintaining Core Values: Even in the face of change, resilience keeps us aligned with our core values, ensuring that trust remains grounded in authenticity. This adaptability allows us to stay true to our principles while being flexible in our approach, keeping relationships healthy and respectful of evolving needs.

Practical Application: Building adaptability in trust situations can involve regular check-ins with trusted individuals, allowing for open discussions around boundaries, expectations, and changes. By actively engaging in these conversations, we create a foundation of trust that adapts to both challenges and growth opportunities.

Adaptability strengthens relationships, allowing trust to **thrive amid change** while keeping us aligned with our highest values.

Creating Trust that is Meaningful and Sustainable

By developing emotional resilience, we cultivate relationships where trust is both **meaningful and sustainable**. This resilience-rooted approach empowers us to trust others without compromising our well-being, supporting connections that are both open and protective of our inner stability.

Empowers Thoughtful Engagement: Emotional resilience enables us to engage in relationships thoughtfully, making intentional decisions around trust that reflect our values. This clarity supports healthier connections, as we are fully present without feeling vulnerable to emotional volatility.

Builds Resilient, Balanced Relationships: Trust grounded in resilience is both steady and adaptable, providing a foundation for relationships that can withstand challenges without shattering. This balanced approach allows us to recover from setbacks, learn from experiences, and trust again with renewed strength.

Aligns with Authentic Values: Resilient trust is aligned with our true values, empowering us to build connections based on principles rather than pressures or expectations. This integrity-driven approach ensures that our relationships are grounded, respectful, and aligned with what matters most.

By cultivating emotional resilience, we create trust that is **empowering, adaptable, and meaningful**. This approach to trust builds connections that honor both our boundaries and our willingness to engage, allowing relationships to flourish in ways that are resilient, authentic, and aligned with our highest values.

8: Practical Tools for Intentional Trust in Complex Settings

In complex settings—whether at work, with family, or in social circles—trust is rarely straightforward. The balance between trust and doubt can be difficult to achieve, especially when motives, expectations, or reliability aren't fully clear. This chapter introduces a **toolkit of practical exercises** designed to help you **place trust intentionally and with self-protection**. By using tools like Trust Tests, Conditional Trust Agreements, and Doubt Verification Checks, you can gradually build trust in complex situations while ensuring that you maintain a healthy balance of openness and caution.

Trust Tests: Building Trust Gradually with Small Commitments

Trust Tests are structured exercises that allow for **gradual trust-building**. Instead of immediately extending full trust, you begin with small, manageable commitments, gauging the person's reliability and responsibility without taking unnecessary risks. Trust Tests provide insight into whether someone is dependable, allowing trust to grow in **measured stages**.

How to Use Trust Tests

Trust Tests help you develop trust based on **observable actions** rather than assumptions. Here's how to use them effectively:

Begin with Low-Stakes Commitments

Starting with a minor responsibility gives you a chance to observe a person's approach to handling commitments without exposing yourself to significant risk.

Example: In a work setting, assign a new team member a small task, such as organizing meeting notes or gathering feedback from the team. This helps you assess their attention to detail, sense of responsibility, and communication skills.

Personal Tip: Choose a task that reflects the skills or traits you're looking to assess, such as punctuality, initiative, or communication. In family settings, this might mean asking a relative to help plan a gathering or run a small errand.

Evaluate Reliability and Consistency

Pay close attention to how the person handles this initial task. Are they prompt, responsible, and communicative? Small commitments provide valuable insight into a person's character and work style, showing you if they're likely to uphold larger responsibilities.

Consider the Following: Did they meet the deadline? Did they communicate openly if challenges arose? How was the quality of their work? These questions help gauge their reliability.

Example: If you notice that a new friend shows up on time, actively engages, and respects boundaries, it might signal they're reliable in other areas too.

Gradually Increase Commitment Levels

If the person successfully fulfills smaller tasks, gradually increase the responsibility level. This incremental approach builds trust on a foundation of **consistent, positive interactions**.

Example: After successfully completing initial tasks, you might ask a new colleague to lead a small part of a team project. If they continue to perform well, you can gradually involve them in more complex or sensitive responsibilities.

Personal Tip: Keep the progression slow and steady, ensuring each step is based on demonstrated reliability. In social settings, you might start by inviting a new friend to informal gatherings and, as trust grows, to more personal events or discussions.

Example Situations for Trust Tests

Trust Tests can be applied in various relationship contexts to build trust gradually:

Work

In professional environments, small tasks allow you to **assess a colleague's commitment and accountability** before involving them in larger projects.

Scenario: You have a new team member and want to assess their skills. Start by asking them to handle a portion of a project, such as drafting an initial outline or summarizing meeting notes. Observe how they approach the task, manage timelines, and communicate updates. If they show reliability, you can gradually entrust them with more significant responsibilities, fostering trust through consistent proof of their abilities.

Family

In family settings, Trust Tests can help rebuild or strengthen connections, particularly if there have been past issues with dependability.

Scenario: Suppose you're reconnecting with a family member who has had past challenges with follow-through. Start by sharing a minor concern or asking for a small favor, such as coordinating a family dinner or assisting with a small household task. Observe their follow-through, respect for boundaries, and willingness to engage. If they demonstrate reliability, you can begin sharing more responsibilities, rebuilding trust in manageable steps.

Social

In social settings, Trust Tests help determine if a new friend or acquaintance is dependable and respects boundaries, allowing the relationship to **develop naturally and authentically**.

Scenario: You've recently connected with someone who seems like a potential friend. Invite them to a small social outing or gathering. Observe their enthusiasm, engagement, and follow-through on plans. If they demonstrate reliability, consider extending more invitations or sharing aspects of your life over time. Each positive interaction reinforces the foundation of trust, allowing the friendship to deepen gradually.

Using Trust Tests to Build Intentional, Discerned Trust

Trust Tests help you approach trust with **intentionality and discernment**. Instead of rushing into trust, you allow it to develop at a pace aligned with real experiences. This approach:

Encourages Measured Trust Growth: Trust Tests prevent you from overcommitting or feeling pressured to trust too quickly. By building trust in stages, you reduce the risk of disappointment or betrayal, fostering relationships that grow at a natural pace.

Builds a Foundation on Reliability: Each successful Trust Test adds another layer of confidence, showing you that the person is dependable through actions rather than words alone. This steady foundation makes it easier to trust confidently in future interactions.

Creates Authentic Connections: Trust Tests ensure that relationships develop based on shared reliability and respect. By observing someone's behavior over time, you create authentic connections that are rooted in mutual accountability and understanding.

With Trust Tests, you cultivate relationships that are resilient, balanced, and based on evidence, allowing trust to grow **gradually and securely**. This tool empowers you to engage in relationships with clarity, reducing risk and allowing for deeper, more meaningful connections based on real experiences.

Conditional Trust Agreements: Setting Clear Expectations and Boundaries

Conditional Trust Agreements establish **clear expectations and responsibilities** within relationships, creating a framework for trust that is **structured, transparent, and secure**. These agreements outline specific conditions for trust and the roles each person will play, which is especially valuable in situations with higher stakes or potential challenges. By defining expectations from the beginning, Conditional Trust Agreements allow both parties to engage with confidence, knowing that trust is guided by mutually understood terms.

How to Use Conditional Trust Agreements

Conditional Trust Agreements are structured to **clarify roles, responsibilities, and boundaries** in relationships. Here's how to implement them effectively:

Define Terms of Trust

Start by outlining the responsibilities, roles, and boundaries of each person in the relationship. This clear definition of terms ensures that everyone knows their specific obligations and understands what is required to maintain trust.

Example: In a family business, this could involve setting terms around who manages finances, who handles client relationships, and how profits are shared. By clarifying these roles, each family member understands their responsibilities, and potential misunderstandings or overstepping are minimized.

Personal Tip: For Conditional Trust Agreements to be successful, the terms should be specific and realistic. It's helpful to consider each person's strengths and areas of expertise when assigning roles, which creates a structure that feels fair and achievable.

Agree on Consequences for Breaches

Specify what will happen if one of the terms is not met. By establishing consequences, you ensure that both parties understand the seriousness of their commitments. Consequences also provide a way to address breaches constructively, allowing trust to be restored if conditions are violated.

Example: In a professional partnership, you might agree that failing to meet deadlines will result in additional oversight or re-evaluation of the partnership. Having pre-defined consequences clarifies the importance of meeting expectations and helps both parties approach the agreement responsibly.

Personal Tip: Consequences should be proportional and constructive rather than punitive. The goal is to create accountability without jeopardizing the relationship. For example, a missed deadline might warrant a follow-up discussion rather than immediate withdrawal from the partnership.

Review and Adjust as Needed

Relationships evolve, and a Conditional Trust Agreement should be flexible enough to reflect these changes. Periodically reviewing the agreement allows both parties to adjust terms, boundaries, or responsibilities as circumstances shift, ensuring that the agreement remains relevant and effective.

Example: In a family caregiving arrangement, if one family member's work schedule changes, revisiting the agreement allows for rebalancing responsibilities. Adjusting the terms maintains fairness, accommodates new needs, and prevents potential strain.

Personal Tip: Schedule regular check-ins to assess the agreement's effectiveness. These reviews foster open communication and create an opportunity to discuss any challenges or areas where the agreement may need updating.

Example Situations for Conditional Trust Agreements

Conditional Trust Agreements are adaptable to various relationship contexts, providing structure and clarity in professional, family, and social settings.

Work

In work or business partnerships, Conditional Trust Agreements can be formalized to **establish clear expectations and provide accountability**.

Scenario: Suppose you're entering a business partnership. A Conditional Trust Agreement can outline each partner's responsibilities, financial contributions, and role in decision-making. Including a conflict resolution clause helps prevent misunderstandings and specifies steps for addressing disagreements constructively, allowing trust to grow within a framework of accountability.

Key Terms: Define who manages finances, deadlines for specific tasks, and who will take the lead on customer relationships. Set consequences for missed deadlines, such as additional oversight or reassignment of roles.

Family

In family settings, Conditional Trust Agreements are especially useful for managing **shared responsibilities** in caregiving or other high-stakes situations.

Scenario: In a family caregiving situation, where multiple family members share responsibilities for a loved one, an agreement can clarify who handles specific tasks (e.g., medical appointments, finances, or daily visits). Conditions might include regular check-ins and equal time contributions, ensuring everyone plays a fair and supportive role.

Key Terms: Specify each person's role, set expectations for how often they'll check in, and agree on a plan for decision-making. Consequences for failing to meet expectations could include reassigning tasks to maintain the arrangement's integrity.

Social

Conditional Trust Agreements can also apply in social situations, where informal agreements can **prevent misunderstandings and preserve friendships**.

Scenario: When planning a shared trip with friends, you can create a conditional agreement covering budgeting, logistics, and shared responsibilities. Clarifying expectations around finances, accommodations, and scheduling helps ensure a smooth trip and reduces the risk of conflicts.

Key Terms: Define each person's financial contribution, agree on who will handle booking and logistics, and establish guidelines for flexibility during the trip. Consequences might include adjustments to individual roles or responsibilities if initial terms aren't met.

Benefits of Conditional Trust Agreements

Conditional Trust Agreements help relationships thrive within **safe, well-defined boundaries.** By clarifying responsibilities and expectations, these agreements create a shared understanding of what trust requires, building a foundation for trust that is both **intentional and secure**.

Prevents Miscommunication and Assumptions: Conditional Trust Agreements clarify expectations from the beginning, ensuring that neither party operates on assumptions. This clarity prevents misunderstandings and keeps the relationship balanced and fair.

Promotes Accountability and Respect: By setting clear terms and consequences, these agreements emphasize accountability, demonstrating that trust requires commitment and respect. Both parties know their roles, responsibilities, and the importance of following through.

Allows Flexibility for Evolving Needs: Relationships aren't static, and Conditional Trust Agreements allow for adjustments over time. By regularly reviewing and updating the terms, you ensure the agreement remains effective and continues to reflect the needs of everyone involved.

Using Conditional Trust Agreements for Long-Term Relationship Success

Conditional Trust Agreements are a **proactive approach to managing trust**, especially in relationships where trust can be impacted by external challenges or evolving responsibilities. By implementing these agreements thoughtfully, you cultivate trust that is **steady, accountable, and adaptable**.

Increases Confidence in Shared Goals: Knowing that each party understands their role and agrees to the terms builds confidence in shared goals. This stability creates a sense of unity, as both parties are aligned on responsibilities and are committed to making the relationship work.

Builds Trust through Action: Conditional Trust Agreements are built on measurable actions rather than vague promises, reinforcing trust through demonstrated commitment and follow-through. Over time, this builds a solid foundation of trust based on reliable behavior.

Encourages Open Communication: By setting up regular reviews, Conditional Trust Agreements foster open communication. Both parties are encouraged to voice concerns, discuss adjustments, and ensure the terms remain fair, which strengthens the relationship's overall resilience.

With Conditional Trust Agreements, you create relationships that are **structured, transparent, and adaptable**, ensuring trust can flourish within boundaries that protect and empower both parties. This approach transforms trust into a dynamic commitment, guided by shared values and mutual respect, enabling relationships to thrive even in complex or high-stakes settings.

Doubt Verification Checks: Using Doubt as a Guide for Trust

Doubt Verification Checks are tools for **evaluating trustworthiness** in a structured, evidence-based way. Rather than dismissing doubt as a barrier, this approach uses doubt as a constructive guide to assess reliability and integrity, especially in complex or ethically ambiguous settings. Doubt Verification Checks encourage you to **verify behaviors and actions objectively**, helping you ground your trust in reality.

How to Use Doubt Verification Checks

Doubt Verification Checks involve a three-step process that transforms uncertainty into constructive observation, allowing you to assess a person's reliability over time. Here's how to put them into practice:

Identify Areas of Doubt

The first step is to **acknowledge specific doubts or uncertainties** about a person or situation. Rather than dismissing or ignoring these feelings, bring them to the surface. By clearly defining areas of doubt, you can direct your focus toward gathering relevant information to address them.

Example: In a new job, you may feel uncertain about a supervisor's transparency regarding team goals. This doubt might inspire you to monitor how openly they share information and if their actions align with what they communicate to the team.

Personal Tip: Make a list of specific concerns or areas where you feel uncertain. By clearly identifying these doubts, you gain a sense of purpose in your observation rather than simply feeling skeptical.

Seek Observable Evidence

Once you've identified areas of doubt, look for **observable evidence** rather than relying on assumptions or verbal assurances. Actions speak louder than words; verifying through actions provides a clearer picture of someone's reliability.

Example: If a colleague promises to keep you updated on a project, note whether they consistently follow through with these updates. Observable actions—such as sharing regular progress reports—offer concrete evidence that supports or contradicts their verbal commitment.

Personal Tip: Track specific behaviors that align with or deviate from what the person has promised. This practice allows you to view their reliability objectively, helping you form an evidence-based perspective rather than relying on assumptions.

Evaluate Patterns over Time

Trust isn't built on a single action or isolated incident. **Look for patterns** in behavior to get a fuller picture of someone's consistency and dependability. Over time, consistent behavior reinforces trust, while inconsistencies might signal the need for cautious engagement.

Example: Suppose a friend makes an effort to stay in touch but cancels plans frequently. Observing this pattern over time—whether they improve or continue the behavior—provides insight into how much trust you can place in their reliability.

Personal Tip: Avoid making immediate judgments based on isolated incidents. Instead, assess behaviors over weeks or months to see if there's a consistent pattern. This patient approach allows trust to grow or evolve naturally, grounded in observable evidence.

Example Situations for Doubt Verification Checks

Doubt Verification Checks can be applied in various settings to help you assess trust in complex relationships:

Work

In the workplace, particularly in new roles or relationships, you may need to assess colleagues' or supervisors' reliability and support without fully knowing their work style. Verification checks can help you gauge whether their actions match their promises.

Scenario: If you're assigned a mentor, but feel uncertain about their availability, observe how regularly they check in and how responsive they are to your questions. If they consistently make time for guidance, this supports trust. If they are often unavailable, it may indicate a need to adjust your expectations.

Outcome: Verification checks allow you to set realistic expectations and engage more confidently, either by building trust if the mentor proves supportive or seeking alternative support if they are inconsistent.

Family

In family relationships, especially with family members who may have a history of unreliability, Doubt Verification Checks can help determine whether you can extend further trust in specific responsibilities.

Scenario: Suppose you have a family member who has struggled to follow through on commitments. Before entrusting them with a significant role—such as organizing a family event—test their reliability by assigning a smaller task, like coordinating part of the setup or managing RSVPs.

Outcome: By observing how they handle this initial responsibility, you gain insight into whether they can be trusted with larger tasks. If they prove reliable, it builds confidence; if not, it helps set boundaries without feeling disappointed.

Social

When building new friendships, you may experience initial doubts about a person's sincerity or reliability. Verification checks can help you assess their commitment to the relationship without assuming trust too quickly.

Scenario: If you're developing a friendship but feel uncertain about the other person's intentions, observe how consistently they initiate contact, follow through on plans, or offer support during important moments. Regular engagement and follow-through indicate their sincerity, while a lack of consistency might prompt caution.

Outcome: This approach allows you to gauge the depth of the friendship based on observable commitment, helping you feel secure about the relationship's direction and potential for growth.

Benefits of Doubt Verification Checks

Doubt Verification Checks help you approach trust in a **structured, observant way**, fostering a realistic and balanced view of others' reliability. By using doubt as a guide rather than a barrier, you create a **proactive, grounded approach to trust**.

Reduces Unnecessary Risks: Verification checks provide a framework for building trust based on evidence, reducing the chance of disappointment or breach. You place trust with discernment, ensuring it aligns with the other person's consistent behavior.

Promotes Objectivity: Relying on observable actions rather than assumptions helps you assess reliability without letting emotions cloud your judgment. This objectivity strengthens your ability to navigate relationships confidently.

Encourages Realistic Expectations: By evaluating patterns over time, you develop a realistic sense of each person's reliability, adjusting your expectations accordingly. This realistic approach reduces the pressure to make immediate judgments, allowing trust to grow naturally.

Using Doubt Verification Checks to Build Intentional Trust

By approaching trust with Doubt Verification Checks, you create relationships where trust is based on **consistent evidence and shared accountability**. This method allows you to engage with others thoughtfully and gradually, ensuring that your trust decisions are aligned with reality.

Develops Confidence in Your Judgments: Verification checks empower you to trust your intuition and observations, providing clarity around who deserves your trust and who may require boundaries.

Builds Resilience in Relationships: Trust grounded in verification is resilient, as it's based on a track record of reliable behavior. You can engage in relationships with confidence, knowing that your trust is backed by evidence rather than assumption.

Supports Adaptability in Complex Situations: Verification checks allow you to adapt your trust level based on observed patterns, making it easier to navigate ethically ambiguous or unpredictable environments without compromising your values.

Using Doubt Verification Checks, you foster relationships that are **authentic, secure, and aligned with reality**. This tool helps you approach trust in a dynamic, thoughtful way, balancing openness with discernment, and ensuring that each trust decision supports your well-being and growth.

Putting the Tools into Practice: Situational Exercises

Applying Trust Tests, Conditional Trust Agreements, and Doubt Verification Checks in real-life scenarios allows you to **build trust gradually, intentionally, and with discernment**. These exercises will help you practice placing trust based on observable actions, clear boundaries, and evidence, creating a balanced and resilient approach to trust in different settings.

Work Scenario

In a workplace setting, especially when managing a new hire or team member, you may feel uncertain about their skills or reliability. Using Trust Tests, Conditional Trust Agreements, and Doubt Verification Checks allows you to build confidence in their abilities while minimizing risk.

Step 1: Start with a Trust Test

Assign the new hire a minor task that has a clear deadline and specific expectations. For example, ask them to compile a report, organize data, or prepare an outline for a project. The task should be low-stakes but meaningful enough to gauge their understanding and commitment.

Objective: Observe their approach to meeting the deadline, their attention to detail, and how well they communicate any questions or challenges that arise.

Step 2: Use Doubt Verification Checks

Without micromanaging, monitor their progress based on observable actions. Check in periodically to see if they provide updates, ask clarifying questions, or inform you of any issues proactively. This verification allows you to assess their reliability without hovering.

Objective: Assess whether their performance aligns with the standards set for the task. If they consistently meet expectations, it demonstrates reliability; if not, it helps you identify areas needing support or additional training.

Step 3: Establish a Conditional Trust Agreement

If the new hire completes the initial task satisfactorily, set up a Conditional Trust Agreement that increases their responsibilities gradually. Outline specific roles and expectations, such as taking ownership of a portion of a larger project. Include regular feedback sessions as part of the agreement to support continuous growth.

Objective: Foster accountability and build trust incrementally, ensuring the new hire feels supported while demonstrating their readiness for greater responsibilities.

Family Scenario

In family dynamics, especially when working with a family member who has been inconsistent in the past, building trust can be challenging. Using a gradual, structured approach with Trust Tests, Doubt Verification Checks, and Conditional Trust Agreements can make trust-building more manageable.

Step 1: Start with a Trust Test

For an upcoming family event, ask the family member to take on a small, low-stakes task, such as managing RSVPs, coordinating one element of the event, or helping with a specific task like ordering supplies.

Objective: Assess their reliability and engagement with the task. Observe how they handle communication and follow-through on their part of the responsibility.

Step 2: Use Doubt Verification Checks

Monitor their follow-through without imposing excessive oversight. Check if they handle the task in a timely manner, respect boundaries, and communicate effectively about any updates or changes.

Objective: Determine if they can manage small commitments reliably. Verification checks allow you to gauge their behavior based on actions rather than assumptions, helping you decide if you can trust them with larger responsibilities.

Step 3: Create a Conditional Trust Agreement

If they prove reliable, establish a Conditional Trust Agreement for the event. Outline roles and expectations clearly for each family member involved, specifying backup plans and contingency options if someone is unable to fulfill their role. This agreement ensures that each person knows their responsibilities and understands the impact of not meeting them.

Objective: Foster accountability and open communication among family members, creating a structured environment where everyone's contributions are clear and supported. This agreement provides a pathway for strengthening family trust without risking the event's success.

Social Scenario

In a new friendship, trust builds slowly as you get to know the other person's character, consistency, and respect for boundaries. Using Trust Tests, Doubt Verification Checks, and informal Conditional Trust Agreements allows you to evaluate the friendship's potential while setting appropriate boundaries.

Step 1: Start with a Trust Test

Invite the new friend to a small social gathering or outing, such as a coffee meet-up, a group event, or a casual dinner. This provides an opportunity to observe how they interact and engage in a low-pressure setting.

Objective: See if they follow through on the plans and how they engage during the outing. Do they show up on time, demonstrate interest, and respect the environment or people around them?

Step 2: Use Doubt Verification Checks

After the initial outing, observe their consistency in keeping in touch, initiating future plans, and engaging with genuine interest. This verification allows you to gauge their commitment without overinvesting too quickly.

Objective: Track their reliability and sincerity based on actions. This helps you discern whether they are likely to respect boundaries and show consistency, giving you a clearer picture of their reliability as a friend.

Step 3: Establish an Informal Conditional Trust Agreement

If the friendship shows promise, discuss boundaries for more personal interactions. For example, agree on respecting each other's privacy, offering support during challenging times, or maintaining open communication about plans. These informal agreements help set expectations around mutual respect and support, which strengthens the friendship gradually.

Objective: Foster a deeper connection with clear boundaries that both parties respect. This approach builds trust without risking vulnerability, helping you feel comfortable and supported as the friendship grows.

Benefits of Practicing with Situational Exercises

These situational exercises provide **real-world applications** for Trust Tests, Conditional Trust Agreements, and Doubt Verification Checks. By practicing these tools, you develop a balanced, adaptable approach to trust that protects your well-being while fostering genuine connections.

Reduces Emotional Risk: Trust grows incrementally, reducing the risk of disappointment or hurt. By starting with small commitments, observing behavior, and setting clear expectations, you avoid premature overinvestment.

Promotes Healthy Boundaries: Conditional Trust Agreements provide a framework that respects each person's needs and limitations, helping you navigate trust with clarity and confidence.

Increases Confidence in Relationships: These tools empower you to engage in relationships with awareness, knowing that trust is backed by real experience and mutual understanding. By following these steps, you become more resilient, adaptable, and confident in your relationships.

Encourages Discernment: Doubt Verification Checks help you manage trust objectively, ensuring that you make decisions based on evidence rather than assumptions or pressure.

Developing a Balanced, Resilient Approach to Trust

Integrating Trust Tests, Conditional Trust Agreements, and Doubt Verification Checks into everyday interactions helps you **navigate trust in complex settings** with intention and protection. These tools allow you to balance openness with caution, fostering connections that are both secure and meaningful.

Practice Discernment: With each trust decision, you gain insight into others' reliability and your own comfort levels, creating a foundation of discernment that helps you build trust gradually.

Strengthen Resilience: By managing trust in stages, you cultivate resilience, knowing you can engage with people without feeling overly vulnerable. Resilience in trust supports your ability to recover from disappointments and maintain healthy boundaries.

Foster Authentic Relationships: These tools promote transparency and mutual respect, helping you build relationships based on consistent actions and shared values.

Through these practical exercises, you develop a framework for **intentional, adaptable trust** that suits a variety of relationships. By combining these tools, you foster a balanced approach to trust that grows through real experiences, empowering you to engage in connections that are resilient, supportive, and aligned with your well-being.

Building Intentional Trust in a Complex World

In a world where motives, reliability, and ethical standards are often ambiguous, navigating trust requires a balanced, intentional approach. Practical tools like **Trust Tests**, **Conditional Trust Agreements**, and **Doubt Verification Checks** equip you to engage in relationships with clarity, confidence, and self-protection. These tools provide a framework that helps you **build trust incrementally and thoughtfully** while ensuring that your well-being and boundaries are respected.

Trust Tests: Building Confidence Gradually

Trust Tests are exercises that help you build trust through small, manageable commitments. Rather than assuming trust right away, you place trust in stages, allowing relationships to develop based on **observable reliability** rather than assumptions.

Gradual Growth: Trust Tests start with low-stakes tasks or responsibilities, giving you a safe way to assess a person's reliability. When someone consistently meets these smaller commitments, it demonstrates their trustworthiness and helps you feel confident in extending more trust.

Building Accountability: By beginning with small commitments, you establish a baseline of accountability that grows as the other person proves reliable. For example, in a new work relationship, a Trust Test could involve asking a colleague to complete a minor task before entrusting them with more significant responsibilities.

Minimizing Risks: Trust Tests reduce emotional and practical risks by allowing you to observe actions over time, ensuring that your investment in the relationship is backed by consistent, positive experiences.

Benefit: Trust Tests provide a method for building trust at a pace that feels comfortable, helping you establish a foundation of confidence and reliability without risking too much too soon.

Conditional Trust Agreements: Structured Expectations for Mutual Respect

Conditional Trust Agreements set clear terms and boundaries, creating **structured expectations** that help both parties understand their roles and responsibilities. These agreements are especially useful in high-stakes situations or relationships where clarity and accountability are essential.

Defined Roles and Boundaries: Conditional Trust Agreements help prevent misunderstandings by explicitly outlining each person's responsibilities and the limits of trust. For instance, in a business partnership, a Conditional Trust Agreement could include specific duties, financial contributions, and timelines for deliverables.

Ensuring Accountability: By specifying consequences for breaches of trust, Conditional Trust Agreements emphasize accountability. This clarity helps both parties understand the significance of their commitments, reinforcing mutual respect and responsibility.

Flexibility for Growth: Relationships evolve, and Conditional Trust Agreements can be reviewed and adjusted as needed. Periodic check-ins allow both parties to reassess the agreement, making adjustments to reflect changes in responsibilities or expectations.

Benefit: Conditional Trust Agreements promote open communication and mutual understanding, creating a framework where trust grows in a structured, respectful environment. This approach fosters a sense of security, allowing both parties to feel supported while honoring each other's boundaries.

Doubt Verification Checks: Mindful Observation for Validation

Doubt Verification Checks use doubt as a constructive guide, allowing you to validate trustworthiness through **mindful observation** rather than blind assumption. This approach is particularly valuable in relationships or environments where ethical standards may be uncertain.

Grounding Trust in Reality: Doubt Verification Checks rely on evidence, using consistent actions rather than verbal promises to assess reliability. By observing behaviors over time, you avoid placing trust prematurely, ensuring that trust is backed by observable proof.

Encouraging Realistic Expectations: This tool helps you set realistic expectations in complex relationships by providing insight into how consistently someone meets commitments. If a person's actions align with their words over time, your confidence in their reliability grows.

Building Resilience: By actively verifying trustworthiness, Doubt Verification Checks allow you to adjust your level of trust in response to real experiences. This adaptability creates a resilient approach to trust, empowering you to engage in relationships without feeling overly vulnerable.

Benefit: Doubt Verification Checks provide a balanced way to navigate trust, allowing you to rely on real evidence rather than assumptions. This mindful approach protects you from potential disappointments while fostering connections based on authenticity.

Bringing It All Together: A Comprehensive Approach to Intentional Trust-Building

Together, **Trust Tests**, **Conditional Trust Agreements**, and **Doubt Verification Checks** offer a comprehensive framework for **building intentional trust**. These tools work together to promote relationships that are both resilient and respectful, enabling you to engage thoughtfully in complex settings.

Trust Tests serve as the starting point, allowing trust to develop gradually through observable actions. This foundation minimizes risks while helping you build confidence in others' reliability.

Conditional Trust Agreements introduce structure, setting clear expectations that ensure accountability and foster mutual respect. By clarifying boundaries, these agreements help both parties feel secure and understood, encouraging long-term trust.

Doubt Verification Checks use doubt as a constructive safeguard, encouraging you to validate trustworthiness through consistency and action. This approach protects you from premature trust while supporting realistic, adaptable relationships.

Fostering Resilient Connections Rooted in Mutual Respect

Incorporating these tools into everyday interactions enables you to build connections that are:

Thoughtfully Placed: Each tool allows you to engage in relationships with intentionality, balancing openness with discernment. This approach protects your well-being while fostering genuine connections.

Flexible and Adaptable: Trust-building isn't static; it evolves as relationships deepen. With these tools, you can adjust your approach based on real experiences, ensuring trust remains grounded in reality.

Empowered by Evidence: By using observable actions and structured agreements, you build trust that is resilient, adaptable, and rooted in respect. These tools empower you to engage meaningfully without feeling overly vulnerable.

Benefit: By integrating Trust Tests, Conditional Trust Agreements, and Doubt Verification Checks, you create a resilient, balanced approach to trust that respects both your boundaries and your capacity for connection.

Intentional Trust-Building for a Complex World

Using practical tools like **Trust Tests**, **Conditional Trust Agreements**, and **Doubt Verification Checks** equips you to build trust intentionally, with doubt as a thoughtful guide. These tools help you navigate complex settings confidently, fostering connections that are authentic, adaptable, and deeply respectful.

Enhanced Self-Protection: Each tool incorporates safeguards that protect your well-being, allowing you to engage in relationships without compromising your emotional security.

Deeper, Authentic Connections: By building trust based on real actions and mutual understanding, you foster relationships that are resilient, enduring, and aligned with shared values.

In a complex world, **intentional trust-building** becomes a pathway to meaningful, balanced relationships. By placing trust thoughtfully, with doubt serving as a gentle guide, you create connections that honor both your needs and your potential for growth, fostering relationships that stand strong amid life's complexities.

9: The Role of Doubt in Ethical Decision-Making

Doubt is often viewed as an obstacle to confidence, but in ethical decision-making, it serves as a powerful ally. Rather than casting doubt as a hindrance, this chapter explores how doubt enables us to **question assumptions, examine situations critically, and make more ethical, informed choices**. In a complex world, where pressures and competing interests often cloud ethical clarity, doubt can guide us to decisions that are rooted in evidence and responsibility. By thoughtfully applying doubt, we can uphold ethical standards even when faced with ambiguity or pressure.

The Power of Doubt in Ethical Decision-Making

In the realm of ethical decision-making, **doubt is not a hindrance** but rather a crucial asset that leads to deeper understanding and integrity. Doubt invites us to pause, reflect, and **examine our assumptions** and the available evidence before acting. By allowing doubt to guide our choices, we cultivate a more thoughtful approach to ethics, one that integrates varied perspectives and anticipates potential outcomes. This active questioning is key to making **well-rounded, ethically responsible decisions** that are aligned with our values and principles.

Questioning Assumptions

Doubt is a powerful tool for **challenging the assumptions** that often shape our decisions unconsciously. We all carry biases, preconceptions, and habitual ways of thinking that can cloud judgment, especially in complex ethical situations. By introducing doubt, we force ourselves to examine whether these assumptions are valid or relevant, ensuring that our decisions are free from unexamined biases.

Example: In a workplace scenario, if there's an assumption that a new initiative will be beneficial based on past successes, doubt can prompt us to question whether the current circumstances are similar to those of previous projects. This leads to a more careful evaluation rather than simply relying on past patterns.

Value: Questioning assumptions helps us avoid hasty conclusions and prevents ethical oversights. It brings a level of intellectual humility to our decision-making process, reminding us that our initial perspectives are not infallible.

How to Apply It: Start by identifying core assumptions within a given decision. Ask, "What am I assuming here? Are these assumptions based on recent evidence, or am I relying on past experiences that may no longer apply?" This questioning process often reveals blind spots and opens the door to more balanced thinking.

Seeking Evidence

Doubt naturally leads to a **search for evidence**. Rather than making decisions based solely on intuition or incomplete information, doubt encourages us to verify facts, seek out alternative viewpoints, and gather data that provides a more complete picture. This evidence-based approach is crucial to making ethical decisions that are defensible, transparent, and rooted in reality.

Example: Suppose a company leader is considering reducing environmental standards to cut costs. By engaging in doubt, they might seek data on the long-term environmental impact, legal risks, and public perception, helping to make a decision that balances financial considerations with social responsibility.

Value: Gathering evidence creates a foundation for responsible decision-making. It minimizes the likelihood of ethical missteps by grounding choices in verified information rather than incomplete perspectives.

How to Apply It: Actively seek multiple sources of information, including expert opinions, research studies, and firsthand observations. Doubt encourages us to ask, "Is there additional information that could either support or challenge this decision? What data can help clarify the potential impacts?"

By rigorously examining the facts, we build trust in our ethical reasoning and make choices that reflect genuine responsibility.

Encouraging Reflective Thinking

Doubt promotes **reflective thinking**, prompting us to consider the ethical dimensions and broader implications of our actions. This reflection allows us to step back and assess our decisions from multiple perspectives, which is especially valuable in situations where competing interests or complex factors are involved.

Example: In a healthcare setting, a doctor may face a dilemma between adhering strictly to hospital protocols and addressing a patient's unique needs. Doubt encourages the doctor to reflect on the ethical priorities of patient care, considering whether an exception could serve the patient better without compromising medical integrity.

Value: Reflective thinking deepens our ethical awareness, helping us anticipate consequences and evaluate the values at stake. Rather than relying on immediate reactions, doubt leads to thoughtful deliberation, making room for a more comprehensive and nuanced approach to decision-making.

How to Apply It: Set aside time to reflect on each decision and its potential impacts. Ask questions like, "What are the ethical implications of this choice? How might it affect all parties involved? Are there alternative actions that could better align with my values?" By considering different angles, reflective thinking enhances our ability to navigate ethical gray areas with integrity and insight.

Doubt as a Mechanism for Ethical Integrity

When applied thoughtfully, doubt becomes a **mechanism for ethical integrity** that steers us toward responsible, values-driven choices. In this way, doubt is not a barrier to confidence; it is a safeguard against rash decisions and an ally in upholding our principles.

Grounding in Values: Doubt pushes us to question whether a decision truly aligns with our core values and ethical standards. This examination helps ensure that our actions are consistent with the principles we want to uphold, even when it's challenging.

Creating Accountability: Doubt introduces a layer of accountability to our decision-making process. By requiring us to verify assumptions and seek evidence, doubt prevents us from making arbitrary choices, reinforcing a commitment to ethical standards that others can trust.

Building Resilience in Ethics: In an uncertain world, doubt builds ethical resilience. When we rely on doubt as a guide, we are better prepared to navigate complex, high-stakes situations without compromising our integrity. This resilience allows us to make decisions that stand up to scrutiny, even in the face of competing interests or external pressures.

Applying Doubt to Make Ethical Decisions

By integrating doubt into our ethical decision-making, we create a system of checks and balances that enhances our ability to act responsibly. Doubt is not about avoiding commitment; it is about making commitments thoughtfully and with integrity. Through doubt, we foster decisions that are:

Balanced and Fair: Doubt allows us to consider all angles and balance the interests of multiple stakeholders, ensuring that our choices are as fair as possible.

Rooted in Responsibility: When doubt guides our choices, we are more likely to accept the consequences of our actions with a sense of ethical responsibility, knowing that we have examined each factor carefully.

Aligned with Principles: Doubt helps us remain true to our values, reminding us to question choices that might deviate from our ethical standards. This alignment creates a stable foundation for decision-making that reflects our highest principles.

Embracing doubt in ethical decision-making is a transformative practice that empowers us to **act with clarity, humility, and a commitment to doing what is right**. By questioning, verifying, and reflecting, we move beyond simple answers and create a pathway to ethical integrity that is resilient and grounded in trust.

Using Doubt to Make Responsible Choices in Complex Ethical Landscapes

In our fast-paced, interconnected world, ethical decision-making often requires navigating layers of complexity, competing interests, and external pressures. In these settings, embracing doubt is a valuable strategy for ensuring that our choices are **thoughtful, responsible, and aligned with our core principles**. Doubt allows us to critically evaluate each factor, avoiding the pitfalls of rash decision-making and enabling us to make choices that reflect integrity and balance.

Slow Down and Question

When we encounter ethical decisions, it can be tempting to respond quickly, especially if there's pressure to act decisively. Doubt, however, serves as a reminder to **slow down and question** each component of the situation. By pausing to analyze each aspect, we can uncover hidden implications and make more informed choices.

Example: Imagine you're working on a project with a tight deadline, and cutting corners on quality control is suggested as a way to meet it. Doubt encourages you to question the implications of this shortcut. How would this decision impact customer satisfaction? What risks might it introduce to the company's reputation? Would this compromise company values on quality and safety?

Guidance: Avoid making choices based on urgency alone. Use doubt to **analyze motivations and examine whether any shortcuts compromise ethical standards**. By questioning each option, you empower yourself to explore alternatives that meet both practical needs and ethical responsibilities. This approach ensures that your decision respects quality, customer trust, and company integrity, rather than sacrificing these for the sake of speed.

Verify Sources and Information

In any decision-making process, particularly in ethically sensitive situations, it's crucial to ensure that **information is accurate and reliable**. Doubt prompts us to scrutinize our sources and verify facts rather than relying on surface-level assumptions or incomplete information. This thorough approach prevents us from being misled and helps us build decisions on a solid foundation.

Example: Suppose a manager suggests bypassing safety protocols to save costs. Doubt allows you to pause and consider the validity of this suggestion. By researching safety data, consulting risk assessments, and reviewing company policies, you can gather objective evidence on the potential consequences. This verification process helps ensure that decisions are grounded in factual data, rather than biased assumptions or incomplete assessments.

Guidance: Practice due diligence by verifying facts from diverse, credible sources. Doubt motivates us to look beyond convenient information, protecting decisions from being influenced by biased claims or partial truths. In ethical decision-making, this attention to detail reduces the risk of overlooking key considerations and enables choices that are transparent, accountable, and well-informed.

Weigh Long-Term Consequences

Doubt encourages us to look beyond immediate benefits and consider the **long-term consequences** of our actions. Ethical decisions are sustainable when they align with enduring values and consider how today's choices might impact the future. By reflecting on these potential outcomes, doubt helps us prioritize decisions that are built on long-term integrity rather than fleeting advantages.

Example: Suppose a company is considering launching a new product that, while innovative, has known flaws. Doubt encourages the company's leaders to pause and think about the long-term repercussions. Could launching this product harm customer trust? Would it negatively impact brand reputation? By evaluating these risks, doubt allows decision-makers to balance the excitement of a new launch with the ethical responsibility to deliver reliable, quality products.

Guidance: Ask whether short-term gains might lead to long-term challenges. Doubt allows us to foresee ripple effects, helping us make choices that stand the test of time and align with both personal and professional values. Ethical decisions are those that, even years later, reflect a commitment to quality, trust, and accountability.

The Ethical Strength of Doubt

Doubt, when used thoughtfully, becomes a tool for ethical strength and clarity. It doesn't slow us down unnecessarily; rather, it ensures that our actions are carefully considered, respectful of all stakeholders, and aligned with the values that define us. Through doubt, we bring rigor, discernment, and integrity to decision-making, allowing us to navigate complex ethical landscapes responsibly.

Encourages Rigorous Examination: Doubt inspires us to scrutinize each component of a decision carefully, uncovering nuances and considering alternative perspectives that might otherwise be missed. This examination leads to decisions that are balanced and thorough.

Reinforces Accountability: By embracing doubt, we take responsibility for validating information and assessing each consequence, promoting a culture of accountability. This approach strengthens our ethical framework, helping us make choices that are transparent and reliable.

Aligns with Core Values: Doubt keeps us grounded in our principles, ensuring that decisions reflect our values. In ethically complex situations, doubt becomes a guiding compass, steering us toward choices that resonate with our commitment to integrity and ethical responsibility.

By using doubt as a guide, we gain the clarity needed to make ethical decisions that are both wise and considerate. In a world filled with complexity, **doubt is the foundation that supports ethical resilience, allowing us to act with purpose, integrity, and respect for all involved**.

Case Studies: Doubt as a Tool for Upholding Ethical Standards

The following case studies illustrate how **constructive doubt** enabled individuals and leaders to make ethical choices in complex, high-stakes environments. In each instance, doubt acted as a catalyst for careful investigation, prompting decisions that were aligned with ethical standards and ultimately led to positive outcomes.

Case Study 1: The Corporate Whistleblower

In a large corporate organization, an employee discovered irregularities in the financial records, noticing discrepancies that suggested potential fraud. At first, they felt uncertain about what to do, knowing that reporting the issue might impact their career or reputation within the company. Doubt about the organization's practices led them to investigate further, carefully gathering evidence and consulting with trusted colleagues to verify their observations.

With a more substantial understanding of the issue, they chose to report their findings to upper management. However, when management failed to address the issue, they escalated the matter to an external regulatory agency. This whistleblowing action ultimately led to an investigation, uncovering widespread unethical activities within the organization and prompting necessary reforms.

Outcome: The employee's decision to trust their doubts and pursue further evidence revealed unethical practices that otherwise might have gone unchecked. By prioritizing integrity over personal convenience, they helped protect shareholders, customers, and the company's reputation in the long run.

Lesson: Doubt can prompt deeper investigation, leading to ethical decisions with wide-reaching positive impacts. In complex or uncertain environments, doubt guides us to seek clarity and transparency, reinforcing ethical integrity even under pressure.

Case Study 2: Healthcare Professional Facing an Ethical Dilemma

In a healthcare setting, a physician was instructed to reduce consultation times to increase patient volume. The new directive conflicted with their commitment to quality care and their belief in spending adequate time with each patient to ensure accurate diagnosis and treatment. Doubting whether this practice aligned with their ethical obligations to patients, they decided to examine the impact that reduced consultation times would have on patient outcomes.

By gathering data on patient satisfaction, treatment accuracy, and health outcomes, they found that shorter consultation times could compromise the quality of care. Equipped with this information, they voiced their concerns to the administration and collaborated to find a balanced solution that allowed the organization to see more patients without sacrificing the quality of care. They suggested efficiency improvements in other parts of the workflow rather than cutting down consultation times directly.

Outcome: The healthcare professional's decision to act on their doubts led to a constructive discussion with the administration. This collaborative approach enabled the organization to increase patient volume without compromising patient care, setting a precedent for ethical healthcare practices within the organization.

Lesson: Doubt encourages professionals to question practices that may compromise ethical standards. By examining the implications of decisions critically, we can find solutions that respect core values even in challenging environments.

Case Study 3: Environmental Policy Decision-Maker

In a government position, an environmental policy advisor was tasked with reviewing a development project that promised economic growth but posed risks to local ecosystems. Although there was considerable pressure from other officials and business leaders to approve the project quickly, the advisor's doubts about the environmental consequences led them to conduct a thorough investigation.

The advisor consulted environmental impact studies, analyzed potential long-term ecological damage, and engaged with community groups to understand their concerns. Their findings revealed that the project could lead to irreversible harm to local ecosystems, which might outweigh the economic benefits in the long run. Based on this information, they advocated for alternative development options that posed less risk to the environment while still supporting economic growth.

Outcome: The advisor's decision to prioritize environmental ethics over quick economic gain led to a more sustainable choice that protected natural resources and respected community interests. This approach supported a balanced view of development that considered environmental responsibility alongside economic goals.

Lesson: Doubt serves as a critical tool for evaluating the ethical implications of decisions with far-reaching impacts. By questioning initial assumptions and seeking a full range of evidence, decision-makers can navigate complex choices responsibly, ensuring that they uphold ethical standards even when under pressure.

Key Takeaways from the Case Studies

These case studies demonstrate how doubt can be a powerful mechanism for upholding ethical standards, enabling individuals to act with integrity even in complex, high-pressure scenarios.

Encourages a Deeper Inquiry: In each case, doubt prompted a closer examination of the situation, helping individuals to go beyond surface-level information. This inquiry led to well-rounded, evidence-based decisions that aligned with ethical principles.

Promotes Accountability and Transparency: Doubt inspires individuals to seek clarity and accountability, especially in environments where ethical standards may be compromised. This approach helps ensure that decisions are made responsibly and transparently.

Balances Competing Pressures: In environments with conflicting interests—such as corporate demands, patient care needs, or economic pressures—doubt serves as a guide to maintain ethical balance. It encourages decision-makers to explore alternatives that satisfy practical requirements without sacrificing integrity.

Protects Long-Term Integrity: The long-term perspective encouraged by doubt allows us to make decisions that hold up over time, creating outcomes that align with ethical standards and contribute to a culture of trust and accountability.

Practical Applications for Using Doubt in Ethical Decision-Making

For those navigating ethical decisions in complex environments, the following practices can help harness doubt constructively:

Conduct Thorough Research: Use doubt as motivation to gather comprehensive information. Consult multiple sources, cross-check facts, and seek input from those who may be impacted by the decision.

Ask Critical Questions: Reflect on each aspect of the decision, questioning assumptions, motivations, and potential consequences. Ask, "Does this choice align with my values?" and "What are the broader impacts of this decision?"

Engage Stakeholders: When doubt arises, engage with stakeholders who may have insights or be affected by the decision. This inclusive approach ensures that diverse perspectives are considered, enriching the decision-making process.

Seek Evidence of Long-Term Impact: Avoid focusing solely on short-term benefits. Use doubt to explore the long-term effects of your decision on the organization, community, and environment, ensuring sustainable and responsible outcomes.

Remain Open to Adjustments: Doubt reminds us to stay flexible and adaptable. If further evidence or feedback suggests that the initial decision may have negative impacts, be willing to make adjustments to uphold ethical standards.

By integrating doubt into decision-making, individuals and leaders can navigate ethical dilemmas with confidence, ensuring that their choices are not only practical but also **consistent with their values and principles**. Embracing doubt in complex environments encourages responsible, transparent actions that support the greater good, fostering a culture of integrity and trust.

Guidance for Embracing Doubt in Ethical Decision-Making

The following practices will help you embrace doubt as a valuable tool in making ethical choices:

Practice Active Listening: When presented with differing perspectives, use doubt to listen carefully to each point of view. This open-minded approach broadens your understanding and helps you consider factors that might otherwise be overlooked.

Consult Multiple Sources: Ethical decisions are best supported by diverse viewpoints. Use doubt to verify information, seek input from trusted advisors, and consider the perspectives of those affected by the decision.

Reflect on Core Values: Reconnect with your ethical values and principles when making decisions. Doubt encourages you to ask, "Does this choice align with my fundamental values?" By staying rooted in your core beliefs, you ensure that your decisions are guided by integrity.

Anticipate Outcomes: Consider the potential impact of your choices on all stakeholders. Doubt helps you evaluate possible consequences, ensuring that your decisions promote long-term well-being rather than short-term convenience.

The Transformative Power of Doubt in Ethical Decisions

When approached thoughtfully, doubt transforms our ethical decision-making, serving as a powerful tool for **integrity, accountability, and trust**. Instead of hindering our confidence, doubt enhances it by encouraging a measured, principled approach to complex choices. By questioning assumptions, verifying evidence, and weighing long-term consequences, doubt steers us toward actions that are both thoughtful and aligned with our highest values. Embracing doubt in this way not only enriches our personal decision-making but also contributes positively to our relationships, organizations, and society as a whole.

Promotes Integrity

Doubt helps us to pause and **reassess our choices against our core values and ethical standards**, reinforcing integrity. In ethical decision-making, it is easy to be swayed by convenience, urgency, or external pressure. However, doubt prompts us to ask critical questions that ensure our actions remain true to our principles, even when it is difficult.

Example: In a high-stakes business decision, doubt may lead us to question whether a profitable option might conflict with customer trust or long-term reputation. By reflecting on our values—such as honesty, fairness, or quality—we can make decisions that uphold integrity rather than seeking only short-term gains.

Value: **Doubt acts as a compass, guiding us back to our principles** when we might otherwise be distracted or swayed. It ensures that our decisions do not simply serve immediate needs but also respect our broader ethical commitments, creating a stronger, more consistent approach to integrity.

Encourages Accountability

Doubt plays a vital role in promoting accountability, as it encourages us to **seek verification and question motivations** before acting. This process guards against shortcuts, biases, or unchecked assumptions that can lead to compromised standards. When we use doubt to verify information, examine evidence, and evaluate each aspect of our decision, we demonstrate a commitment to accuracy and transparency.

Example: In a workplace setting, doubt might lead a manager to verify the fairness of a performance review process. By questioning whether all team members are evaluated consistently and without bias, they ensure that their decisions are based on merit rather than favoritism or assumptions.

Value: **Doubt cultivates a mindset of responsibility and diligence**. By approaching decisions with accountability, we create outcomes that withstand scrutiny, reduce the likelihood of unintended harm, and build a culture where ethical standards are upheld consistently. This approach builds trust within teams, organizations, and communities, showing that decisions are made responsibly and transparently.

Builds Trust in Complex Environments

In environments where ethical standards may not always be clear, doubt serves as a **foundation for building trust**. When we allow doubt to inform our decisions, it demonstrates to others that we prioritize careful, responsible choices over impulsive actions. This commitment to thoughtful decision-making fosters trust, as others recognize that we are guided by a dedication to ethical integrity and fairness.

Example: In a community project involving multiple stakeholders, doubt may prompt a leader to regularly seek feedback, verify outcomes, and ensure transparency in financial reporting. By doing so, they build trust among participants and stakeholders, who see that the project is managed with integrity and respect for all involved.

Value: **Doubt strengthens relationships by reinforcing trust and transparency**. When others see that we make decisions with care and responsibility, they are more likely to feel secure in our leadership or partnership. This trust not only facilitates smoother collaboration but also cultivates a culture of openness and mutual respect.

Embracing Doubt for Thoughtful Ethical Decision-Making

Doubt, when embraced as a tool rather than a hindrance, enriches our capacity for **responsible, thoughtful choices**. It serves as a reminder to approach each decision with curiosity, caution, and an unwavering commitment to ethical integrity. By integrating doubt into our decision-making process, we achieve the following transformative outcomes:

Enhanced Clarity: Doubt encourages us to look deeper, clarify our motives, and evaluate the long-term impact of our choices. This clarity allows us to approach each decision from a place of authenticity, aligning our actions with our values.

Stronger Ethical Foundation: When we use doubt to verify, question, and reflect, we develop a stronger ethical foundation, one that prioritizes integrity and accountability over convenience or expedience.

Contribution to a Just, Thoughtful World: As we adopt doubt as a guide, our decisions not only benefit our personal growth and relationships but also contribute positively to society. In embracing doubt, we foster a culture of careful consideration, respect, and ethical responsibility that can inspire others to approach decision-making thoughtfully.

A Commitment to Integrity Through Doubt

In embracing doubt, we commit to a process of **constant ethical reflection and growth**. Rather than acting impulsively or taking ethical standards for granted, doubt encourages us to actively maintain integrity, accountability, and trust as guiding principles in all aspects of life. Through doubt, we can uphold ethical principles that benefit both ourselves and the world around us, creating decisions that are resilient, principled, and deeply aligned with the values we wish to uphold.

Ultimately, **the transformative power of doubt** lies in its ability to connect us to our ethical core, guiding us to act with purpose, clarity, and respect. By making doubt an intentional part of our decision-making process, we create choices that resonate with integrity and compassion, leading to a more thoughtful, just, and trustworthy world.

10: Trust and Doubt as Partners—Creating a Personal Philosophy

In an ever-changing, ethically ambiguous world, the relationship between trust and doubt is crucial for navigating relationships and decisions with both openness and caution. Trust alone can sometimes feel naïve, while doubt alone may seem overly skeptical. By integrating the two, however, we can create a personal philosophy that embraces both trust and doubt as complementary forces. This balanced approach empowers us to **trust thoughtfully, doubt constructively, and act confidently** in even the most complex situations.

This chapter invites you to develop your own **personal philosophy of trust**, one that allows you to engage in relationships and decisions with both heart and discernment. By trusting with caution, using doubt as a filter, setting clear boundaries, and relying on verification, you can cultivate an approach to trust that is adaptable, resilient, and aligned with your values.

Developing a Personal Philosophy of Trust and Doubt

Creating a personal philosophy of trust provides you with a **framework to navigate relationships and decisions thoughtfully**. It offers guidance on how, when, and to what extent you choose to extend trust, and it encourages you to use doubt constructively to safeguard your well-being. This philosophy is grounded in self-awareness, balance, and an understanding of your core values, allowing you to engage in the world with confidence and integrity.

A personal philosophy of trust is **not a rigid set of rules** but an adaptable mindset that evolves over time. Trust is not a simple, one-time decision; it's a dynamic process influenced by experiences, people, and situations. By developing this philosophy, you empower yourself to embrace trust and doubt as complementary forces, finding a balanced approach between **blind trust and excessive skepticism**. This balance helps you engage meaningfully with others while preserving your integrity and protecting your boundaries.

Why Develop a Personal Philosophy of Trust?

In a world where ethical standards are often complex or unclear, a personal philosophy of trust allows you to **approach decisions with clarity and confidence**. It serves as a personal code, guiding you to make choices that align with your values and respect your boundaries. Developing this philosophy helps you:

Act with Intentionality: A clear philosophy allows you to extend trust with purpose rather than out of obligation or habit. It reminds you to engage thoughtfully, basing your decisions on a conscious assessment of each relationship or situation.

Balance Openness with Self-Protection: By defining boundaries, your philosophy offers a way to balance openness with caution, allowing you to trust without becoming overly vulnerable. It gives you a roadmap for engaging with trust responsibly and discerningly.

Strengthen Self-Awareness and Resilience: Reflecting on trust and doubt cultivates self-awareness, helping you understand what matters most to you in relationships and decisions. This self-awareness supports resilience, as you become more attuned to your needs, boundaries, and values.

Elements of a Personal Philosophy of Trust

Creating a personal philosophy of trust involves **several key elements** that guide how you extend trust, use doubt, and set boundaries. These elements provide a foundation for making choices that feel authentic, balanced, and ethically aligned.

Defining When and How to Trust

Your philosophy begins with defining the circumstances under which you feel comfortable extending trust. This involves assessing relationships, responsibilities, and settings to determine when trust is appropriate and how it should be given. It's a thoughtful approach to trust that avoids extremes and values context.

Questions to Consider:

✓ What qualities or actions make me feel comfortable trusting someone?

✓ How do I decide which people or situations are worth my trust?

✓ Under what circumstances am I willing to extend trust more freely, and when do I hold back?

Application: For example, in professional relationships, you may decide to trust coworkers with smaller tasks initially, observing their reliability before delegating larger responsibilities. In personal relationships, you might choose to share selectively until mutual understanding and respect are demonstrated consistently.

Using Doubt as a Constructive Tool

Doubt is a powerful part of your trust philosophy, as it helps you assess each situation critically and protect yourself from potential risks. Rather than seeing doubt as an obstacle, you can embrace it as a **guide that ensures trust is extended mindfully**. Doubt becomes a way to verify intentions, confirm reliability, and maintain boundaries without closing yourself off from meaningful connections.

Questions to Consider:

✓ How do I recognize when doubt is valid and should be taken seriously?

✓ How can I use doubt constructively without becoming overly suspicious or guarded?

✓ In what ways can doubt act as a reminder to verify information or observe actions before making a decision?

Application: In a business partnership, doubt might lead you to verify a new partner's financial history or seek references before committing. In friendships, doubt could encourage you to observe whether someone follows through on their promises, helping you build trust based on actions rather than assumptions.

Setting and Communicating Boundaries

Boundaries are the framework that **protects your well-being and defines the limits of your trust**. They help you to stay true to your values while engaging meaningfully with others. Setting boundaries is an act of self-respect, ensuring that trust is extended in ways that honor your needs and values.

Questions to Consider:

✓ What boundaries do I need to feel safe and respected in my relationships?

✓ How do I communicate these boundaries to others in a way that feels clear and assertive?

✓ In what situations am I willing to adjust my boundaries, and when do they remain non-negotiable?

Application: In a family relationship, setting boundaries might mean clearly defining areas where you feel comfortable seeking support and areas that remain private. In a professional setting, boundaries could involve defining responsibilities in a collaborative project to ensure accountability and reduce misunderstandings.

Relying on Verification and Observation

Verification is an essential component of a trust philosophy, as it allows you to observe actions rather than relying solely on promises. By incorporating verification, you create a **grounded, realistic approach to trust** that protects you from disappointment while still allowing trust to grow over time.

Questions to Consider:

✓ What forms of evidence or verification do I need before extending deeper trust?

✓ How can I practice observing actions rather than simply accepting words or promises?

✓ In which relationships or settings is verification most important to ensure accountability?

Application: In a mentorship relationship, verification might involve setting regular check-ins to confirm progress. In social settings, you could choose to observe how a new friend supports you during difficult times before confiding in them about personal matters.

Trust as an Art Form: Flexibility and Adaptation

A personal philosophy of trust is not rigid; it is a **dynamic process that adapts to different relationships, situations, and stages of life**. Trust is an art that balances openness with self-protection, changing as you grow, learn, and experience new relationships. By embracing this art form, you can cultivate trust that is responsive to the complexities of today's world while remaining true to your values.

Flexibility in Approach: Trust may look different in various settings—what works in professional relationships may not apply to personal connections. Allow your philosophy to reflect these nuances, adjusting your approach based on the needs of each unique situation.

Adaptation Through Experience: As you encounter new people, challenges, and environments, your philosophy will naturally evolve. Past experiences may reveal areas where you need stronger boundaries or encourage you to trust more fully in certain contexts. Trust is a journey, not a fixed state, and your philosophy should reflect that adaptability.

Crafting Your Personal Philosophy of Trust and Doubt

Developing this philosophy involves a process of self-reflection, practice, and fine-tuning. Consider the following steps as you craft a philosophy that is both meaningful and sustainable:

Identify Core Values: Start by clarifying the values that you want your trust philosophy to reflect—such as honesty, respect, accountability, or compassion. These values will guide each element of your philosophy.

Reflect on Past Experiences: Think about times when trust served you well and times when it did not. Identify what these experiences taught you about setting boundaries, using doubt, and verifying actions. Use these lessons to inform your philosophy.

Practice Mindful Trusting: Apply your philosophy gradually in real-life settings, starting with low-stakes relationships or responsibilities. As you gain confidence, adapt your approach to fit more complex or high-stakes situations.

Reassess and Evolve: Revisit your philosophy regularly to ensure it remains aligned with your goals, experiences, and personal growth. Adjust as needed, allowing it to evolve naturally as you encounter new situations and insights.

Creating a Balanced Path Forward

A personal philosophy of trust that integrates doubt as a partner allows you to engage with the world meaningfully and responsibly. This approach empowers you to make connections that are grounded in mutual respect, transparency, and accountability. By cultivating trust as an art form, you can navigate even the most challenging ethical landscapes with integrity and confidence.

In a world where ethical clarity is not always guaranteed, a balanced trust philosophy is an invaluable tool. It reminds you that **trust and doubt are not opposing forces but complementary guides** that, together, can lead to resilient, authentic relationships. Through this philosophy, you engage with a balanced openness that honors both your trust and your inner wisdom, creating a path that reflects your highest values and aspirations.

Key Principles of a Balanced Trust Philosophy

In a complex world, a balanced trust philosophy integrates both trust and doubt as complementary forces. This approach allows you to engage with openness while protecting your well-being. The following principles offer a foundation for trust that is intentional, adaptable, and aligned with your core values.

Trusting with Caution

Trusting with caution is about extending trust **incrementally** rather than placing immediate, full confidence in someone or something. Especially in situations where motives or intentions are not entirely clear, cautious trust allows you to **stay open while managing risk**.

Why It Matters: Exercising caution helps you protect yourself from emotional and practical overextension. This careful approach enables you to observe actions and patterns over time, creating a foundation of trust that is built on consistency rather than assumptions. Trusting gradually provides you with a sense of security and resilience, as you're less likely to experience sudden disappointment or betrayal.

Practical Application: Trusting with caution could mean starting with low-stakes commitments. For example, you might share minor responsibilities with a new team member before delegating larger tasks, or share casual information with a new friend before confiding personal matters. This incremental approach allows you to observe patterns of reliability and build trust based on real experiences rather than initial impressions.

Using Doubt as a Filter

Doubt, when used as a filter, becomes a **constructive tool** that helps you assess intentions, verify actions, and set appropriate boundaries. Instead of allowing doubt to prevent trust, using it as a filter enables you to engage thoughtfully and responsibly.

Why It Matters: Doubt encourages you to ground your trust in reality rather than assumptions or incomplete information. By asking questions and seeking clarity, doubt helps you avoid missteps and prevents you from placing trust where it may not be warranted. Doubt as a filter is a form of self-protection, allowing you to interact meaningfully while safeguarding your own well-being.

Practical Application: Using doubt as a filter might involve checking references, verifying claims, or consulting feedback from others. For instance, if a colleague with a history of missing deadlines promises timely delivery, doubt would prompt you to ask for regular updates rather than relying solely on their assurance. In friendships, doubt might guide you to observe consistency before assuming someone's loyalty, allowing trust to build naturally.

Setting Boundaries

Boundaries are **essential guardrails** that define the extent and limits of your trust. By setting clear boundaries, you protect your well-being and prevent trust from leading to over-dependence or vulnerability. Boundaries offer clarity for both yourself and others, reducing misunderstandings and fostering respect.

Why It Matters: Boundaries help you engage in relationships without compromising your values, emotional health, or sense of self. By clearly defining what you are willing to share, delegate, or commit to, boundaries ensure that trust is given in ways that are sustainable. Boundaries also promote mutual respect, as they communicate your needs and expectations in a way that others can understand and honor.

Practical Application: Setting boundaries could involve limiting the amount of personal information you share with someone new, establishing professional limits in a work setting, or clearly defining roles in a collaborative project. For example, you may choose to share work-related tasks with colleagues but maintain privacy around personal matters, or in a family setting, establish boundaries that protect your time and energy.

Relying on Verification

Verification is the practice of **observing actions, seeking evidence, and assessing consistency**. Rather than relying solely on promises or stated intentions, verification allows you to build trust based on concrete, reliable actions over time. This principle ensures that trust is grounded in observable reality.

Why It Matters: Verification strengthens trust by transforming it into something tangible and resilient. When trust is based on actions rather than assumptions, you are less susceptible to disappointment or disillusionment. Verification empowers you to trust wisely, using evidence to inform your decisions rather than leaving them to chance.

Practical Application: Verification might involve setting up regular check-ins in a professional setting, reviewing results, or using feedback mechanisms to ensure that commitments are being met. For instance, if you delegate a project, regular progress reports can serve as a form of verification, confirming that responsibilities are being upheld. In personal relationships, verification could mean observing how consistently someone follows through on their commitments before deepening the level of trust.

Bringing It All Together: A Balanced Philosophy of Trust

By integrating these principles, you create a personal trust philosophy that is grounded, adaptable, and resilient. Trust becomes a dynamic process, one that allows you to engage meaningfully with the world without losing your sense of self or compromising your values.

Stay Open Yet Mindful: Allow yourself to trust others while using caution, doubt, boundaries, and verification as tools that ensure this trust is well-placed. This balance prevents you from being overly skeptical or overly trusting, enabling relationships that feel safe and authentic.

Adapt to Different Situations: Trusting with caution and verification might be more necessary in professional settings, while personal relationships may rely more on boundaries and gradual trust-building. Flexibility allows your trust philosophy to respond to the unique needs of each context.

Evolve with Experience: Trust and doubt are influenced by experience and change over time. Regularly revisit your approach to trust as you grow, learn, and encounter new relationships or challenges. Allow yourself to adjust boundaries or verification measures as needed, reflecting your current values and insights.

By embracing trust as both an art and a balance between openness and self-protection, you develop a philosophy that is both robust and adaptable. Trusting thoughtfully, questioning carefully, and setting clear boundaries give you a powerful framework for creating connections that are meaningful, grounded, and deeply aligned with your core values.

Integrating Trust and Doubt: A Balanced Approach

A balanced approach to trust embraces both **trust and constructive doubt** as essential partners. This philosophy offers a middle path, allowing you to engage meaningfully in relationships without becoming overly vulnerable or developing unrealistic expectations. By allowing doubt to act as a guide, you make intentional choices rooted in discernment and self-protection. This balanced mindset empowers you to approach each situation with clarity and confidence, adapting as circumstances shift.

Stay Open Yet Mindful

Remaining open to connections and opportunities is essential for growth, yet allowing doubt to prompt careful consideration keeps this openness grounded. Staying open-minded does not mean blindly trusting everyone or every situation; instead, it encourages **thoughtful engagement**.

Why It Matters: By combining openness with mindfulness, you foster a sense of curiosity and receptivity without compromising your boundaries. This approach helps you remain aware of potential red flags or signals that may suggest caution, ensuring that you're not swept into situations where trust might be unwarranted.

Practical Application: In new relationships, staying open might mean engaging fully in conversations or shared activities while being attentive to patterns of behavior. If inconsistencies or red flags appear, you can address them without immediately closing yourself off. For example, in a professional setting, you might be open to collaborating with a new team member but use doubt as a reminder to review their work carefully, especially if you're unfamiliar with their reliability.

Staying open yet mindful fosters a **middle ground where trust can grow** at a natural pace, guided by both genuine interest and discernment.

Adjust as Needed

Trust and doubt are not fixed; they are influenced by experience, context, and changing dynamics. As new information or experiences come to light, **adjusting your level of trust** ensures that your approach remains relevant and responsive. Flexibility is essential to prevent rigidly holding onto assumptions or expectations that may no longer be valid.

Why It Matters: Adjusting your trust level as situations evolve helps prevent disappointment and allows you to align your trust with reality. This flexibility fosters resilience by making room for learning and adaptation, allowing trust to grow when justified or retract when needed.

Practical Application: In friendships, you might start with moderate trust and gradually increase it as consistency and reliability are demonstrated. Alternatively, if a close friend repeatedly fails to respect boundaries, you can reduce trust while maintaining the connection. Similarly, in a work project, if a team member who was initially unreliable improves their communication and accountability, you might increase trust in their contributions.

Adjusting trust as needed helps you stay attuned to the **natural rhythms of relationships**, allowing for healthy, balanced connections.

Embrace Trust as an Art

Trust is not a one-size-fits-all approach; it's an art form that adapts to different situations, personalities, and dynamics. Approaching trust as an art requires flexibility, intuition, and the **willingness to navigate ambiguity**. It's a skill that can be honed over time, shaped by both intuition and experience.

Why It Matters: Viewing trust as an art encourages you to approach relationships with a sense of curiosity and creativity. It allows you to navigate complex or ethically ambiguous situations with confidence, recognizing that trust may look different in each context. By embracing trust as an evolving, flexible process, you create space for authentic, resilient connections.

Practical Application: In a new social group, you may decide to trust selectively by engaging in casual conversations and observing dynamics before sharing personal information. With family, you might deepen trust gradually by sharing milestones and seeking support on specific matters. Viewing trust as an art allows you to navigate diverse interactions, adapting your approach based on each relationship's unique rhythm and needs.

Embracing trust as an art allows you to **honor the individuality of each relationship** while remaining true to your core values and self-protection.

Creating a Resilient, Intentional Approach to Trust

By integrating trust and doubt, you create a philosophy that is both **grounded and adaptable**. This balanced approach to trust becomes a valuable tool, enabling you to engage in relationships that are both fulfilling and secure. It encourages you to:

Cultivate Openness with Boundaries: Being open to connection while using doubt to establish boundaries ensures that you stay engaged without compromising your needs.

Adapt Based on Experience: As relationships grow or evolve, adjusting your approach to trust ensures that it remains relevant and responsive, reinforcing the foundation of each connection.

Approach Trust as a Lifelong Skill: Trust is a dynamic process that requires constant refinement. By viewing trust as an art, you empower yourself to approach it with a sense of play, curiosity, and wisdom, making it a skill that deepens over time.

This balanced approach allows you to **build resilient, meaningful relationships** where trust is grounded in discernment and aligned with your values. By integrating trust and doubt, you cultivate a trust philosophy that is adaptable, empowering, and deeply rooted in self-awareness, helping you navigate complex relationships with grace and integrity.

Creating Your Personal Trust Philosophy

A personal trust philosophy is a guiding framework that aligns your approach to trust with your values, boundaries, and lived experiences. By intentionally building this philosophy, you empower yourself to make thoughtful, balanced choices that foster healthy relationships and protect your well-being. Below are steps to help you develop a trust philosophy that resonates deeply with who you are and how you wish to engage with others.

Reflect on Your Values

Your trust philosophy begins with understanding the values that guide your life and relationships. **Identifying core values** provides clarity and a foundation upon which to base your decisions about trust.

Why It Matters: Values serve as the compass for your actions and decisions. When your trust decisions reflect your values, they feel authentic and aligned, reducing inner conflict and fostering meaningful connections.

How to Reflect: Take time to identify values that matter most to you in relationships—honesty, integrity, respect, reliability, or empathy, for example. Ask yourself, *"What principles do I want my trust decisions to reflect?"* Reflect on past experiences where trust aligned or conflicted with these values, and note what felt right or wrong about those situations.

Example: If reliability and honesty are core values, you might choose to build trust gradually, allowing actions to demonstrate reliability before fully investing in the relationship. Aligning with these values helps you stay true to your standards.

Define Boundaries and Limits

Boundaries are the **guardrails of your trust philosophy**. By clarifying what you're comfortable sharing, delegating, or committing to in different relationships, you can protect your well-being while staying open to connection.

Why It Matters: Boundaries help you trust without overextending yourself. They provide a clear framework for engagement, preventing burnout or emotional exhaustion by defining where trust begins and ends in each context.

How to Define: Think about where you feel safe or vulnerable when extending trust. Define what you're comfortable sharing in new relationships versus established ones, and clarify areas where you need more caution. Ask yourself questions like, *"What am I willing to invest in this relationship?"* and *"What are my deal-breakers?"*

Example: In a professional setting, boundaries might mean sharing work-related responsibilities but keeping personal details private. In personal relationships, it could involve being selective with your confidences and gradually opening up as mutual respect and understanding grow.

Practice Gradual Trust-Building

Trust does not have to be immediate; **gradual trust-building** allows you to observe and assess others' reliability over time. By taking small steps, you protect yourself from unnecessary risk and allow trust to develop naturally.

Why It Matters: Building trust gradually prevents emotional or practical over-investment in relationships that may not meet your standards. This approach fosters trust based on consistent actions, reinforcing a sense of security and reducing the likelihood of disappointment.

How to Practice: Start by sharing minor responsibilities or information, and observe how others respond. Look for consistency in their actions and integrity over time before moving forward with deeper trust.

Example: In a new friendship, begin with casual gatherings and simple conversations, observing how the person responds and interacts. As you see signs of reliability and empathy, consider sharing more personal thoughts, allowing the friendship to deepen based on real experiences rather than assumptions.

Use Doubt Constructively

Doubt is an **important tool for self-protection and discernment** in trust decisions. Instead of letting doubt close you off from new connections, use it to prompt thoughtful verification and reflection.

Why It Matters: Constructive doubt helps prevent hasty decisions and encourages a balanced approach to trust. By viewing doubt as a healthy reminder to observe actions and verify intentions, you maintain a sense of agency over your trust decisions.

How to Use Doubt: Let doubt prompt you to seek evidence, verify claims, or observe patterns over time. Use doubt as a guide for checking in with yourself and assessing whether trust is warranted, rather than as a reason to withdraw or distrust entirely.

Example: If a colleague promises to support you in a new project but you feel uncertain based on past experiences, doubt might prompt you to request regular check-ins to verify their commitment. This way, doubt helps you ensure that the trust you place in them is based on real follow-through rather than assumptions.

Regularly Reassess

Your trust philosophy is a **dynamic, evolving framework** influenced by life experiences, relationships, and personal growth. Regularly revisiting and refining your philosophy allows it to adapt to your changing needs and insights.

Why It Matters: As you grow and encounter new situations, your approach to trust may need to shift to remain relevant and effective. By reassessing regularly, you allow your philosophy to evolve, ensuring it reflects your current values, boundaries, and experiences.

How to Reassess: Set aside time periodically to review your trust philosophy. Reflect on recent trust decisions and assess whether they felt aligned with your values. Consider what you've learned from recent experiences and make adjustments to your boundaries or approach if necessary.

Example: After navigating a challenging work project, you might realize that you prefer more structured verification in collaborative settings. Adjusting your trust philosophy to include more checkpoints in future projects allows you to continue trusting responsibly in line with your current needs.

Crafting a Resilient and Flexible Trust Philosophy

Creating a personal trust philosophy is an ongoing journey. It requires regular reflection, adaptability, and a willingness to learn from each experience. This philosophy is not a rigid set of rules but a **fluid, adaptable guide** that evolves with you, supporting your ability to navigate relationships confidently and ethically.

By embracing values, boundaries, gradual trust-building, constructive doubt, and reassessment, you create a trust philosophy that:

Reflects Your Authentic Self: By grounding your philosophy in your core values, you ensure that each trust decision aligns with who you are and what you stand for.

Protects Your Well-Being: Setting clear boundaries and practicing gradual trust-building allows you to engage in relationships that feel safe, meaningful, and empowering.

Fosters Meaningful Connections: By using doubt constructively and adjusting as needed, you create a trust approach that respects the uniqueness of each relationship and its evolving dynamics.

This balanced, thoughtful approach enables you to **trust with discernment** and **connect with authenticity**, empowering you to create relationships that are resilient, adaptable, and aligned with your highest values. Through this philosophy, you engage with the world thoughtfully, embracing trust as an art form that adapts and deepens as you grow.

Inspiring Resilience Through Trust and Doubt

A personal philosophy that weaves together trust and doubt is both **practical and empowering**. It allows you to engage in relationships and complex situations with resilience, fostering a type of trust that is **intentional, adaptable, and deeply rooted in integrity**. This approach not only strengthens your own sense of security but also builds a foundation for meaningful connections and a legacy that impacts others positively.

Finding Strength in Balance

By viewing trust and doubt as complementary, you discover a **balance that nurtures both connection and self-protection**. Embracing this balance means that you can engage fully in relationships without losing your sense of self or compromising your emotional well-being.

Why It Matters: Balancing trust and doubt prevents you from veering toward extremes—either blind trust or complete distrust. This balanced approach offers a middle ground that enables you to invest in relationships and situations thoughtfully, with a clear sense of your boundaries. It empowers you to trust without the fear of emotional compromise or vulnerability.

Practical Insight: When trust and doubt coexist, they create a dynamic support system. Trust allows you to open up and connect with others, while doubt encourages you to observe, verify, and adjust your approach as needed. This interplay fosters resilience, giving you the strength to adapt to challenges and uncertainties in relationships.

Example: In professional collaborations, trust enables you to work cohesively, while doubt reminds you to set checkpoints or follow up on responsibilities. This balanced approach strengthens your role in the team and fosters an environment of mutual accountability and respect.

Fostering Meaningful Connections

A philosophy that combines trust and doubt **encourages relationships that are genuine and intentional**. Rather than diving into connections without forethought, you allow trust to develop gradually, based on shared values, consistent actions, and mutual respect. This approach nurtures relationships that are deeply meaningful and grounded in authenticity.

Why It Matters: Relationships built on a foundation of balanced trust are more likely to endure because they are rooted in truth and mutual respect. By allowing trust to grow intentionally, you avoid the pitfalls of superficial or unsustainable connections, fostering bonds that can adapt and thrive over time.

Practical Insight: Intentional trust-building encourages open communication, shared values, and reciprocal respect. This approach ensures that each connection develops at a pace that feels safe and fulfilling, creating relationships that enrich your life without emotional risk.

Example: In a new friendship, instead of immediately sharing personal information, you might engage in shared activities or casual conversations. Over time, as your friend demonstrates consistency and reliability, trust deepens naturally, creating a meaningful connection based on authenticity rather than assumption.

Building a Legacy of Integrity

Cultivating a balanced trust philosophy also means that you are **leaving a legacy of integrity**. This legacy influences not only your own life but also the lives of those around you. When others witness your approach to trust—with caution, openness, and ethical responsibility—they are encouraged to adopt a similar approach, promoting a culture of thoughtful and responsible trust.

Why It Matters: A legacy of integrity contributes to environments that value ethical responsibility, honesty, and accountability. This approach not only strengthens your relationships but also serves as a positive influence on colleagues, family members, and friends, encouraging them to approach trust with mindfulness and integrity.

Practical Insight: Acting as a role model for balanced trust means demonstrating how trust can coexist with doubt, fostering resilience and ethical behavior in complex situations. When others see you building trust responsibly, they are more likely to feel inspired to approach their own relationships with the same level of intentionality.

Example: In a leadership role, setting boundaries, verifying commitments, and maintaining transparency can inspire team members to engage in similar practices. Your approach creates a culture where trust is respected, accountability is valued, and everyone feels empowered to build ethical, resilient relationships.

The Resilience of a Balanced Trust Philosophy

By integrating trust and doubt, you build a personal philosophy that is adaptable, resilient, and empowering. This balanced approach to trust strengthens your ability to face complex situations with confidence, creating a foundation for personal growth, meaningful connections, and a life led with integrity.

Strength in Flexibility: Balancing trust and doubt gives you the flexibility to adapt as situations evolve, strengthening your ability to handle changes and challenges with resilience.

Authentic Relationships: By approaching trust intentionally, you cultivate relationships that are both secure and meaningful, grounded in mutual respect and shared values.

A Legacy of Integrity: As you practice balanced trust, you build a legacy that promotes ethical, responsible, and thoughtful relationships. This legacy contributes to a world where trust is given wisely, sustained with integrity, and valued deeply.

In embracing this approach, you turn trust and doubt into **powerful partners** that guide you in navigating a complex world with resilience, self-awareness, and integrity. Through this philosophy, you empower yourself and inspire others, leaving a lasting impact that extends beyond individual relationships to create a ripple effect of thoughtful, empowered trust.

Trust as an Art Form in an Unethical World

In a world where ethical standards are not always clear, trust is no longer a simple, unquestioned choice; instead, it becomes an **art form** that requires discernment, adaptability, and resilience. This nuanced approach to trust acknowledges that not every individual or institution will act with integrity, and yet it refuses to fall into cynicism or excessive doubt. By developing a **personal philosophy that combines trust with constructive doubt**, you create a way of navigating relationships that is both thoughtful and protective, fostering connections that are meaningful, secure, and aligned with your values.

Trust as a Mindful Practice

In a complex and sometimes unethical world, trust becomes a **mindful practice**—one that involves a series of intentional choices rather than a one-time decision. This approach honors the uncertainties and potential risks in relationships while making space for genuine connection.

Why It Matters: When trust is approached as a mindful practice, you remain fully present in your relationships, balancing openness with self-protection. It allows you to appreciate the positive aspects of connection without being blindsided by unrealistic expectations or assumptions about others' intentions.

Example: In a new workplace, rather than immediately assuming trust or mistrust, you might start by observing how your colleagues interact, following up on commitments, and gradually sharing information. This careful approach to trust reflects a mindfulness that builds connections on solid ground rather than wishful thinking.

A Philosophy That Merges Trust and Doubt

A trust philosophy that merges trust and doubt allows you to **navigate relationships with clarity and intentionality**. This balanced approach to trust doesn't mean skepticism or naivety; it's a way of understanding that both trust and doubt can coexist as powerful allies. Trust opens the door to connection, while doubt acts as a **guide for discernment**.

Why It Matters: When trust and doubt are combined, they create a framework for making choices that protect your well-being and honor your values. This balanced perspective gives you confidence to engage meaningfully in relationships without fear of betrayal or emotional compromise.

Example: In personal relationships, merging trust with doubt might mean allowing yourself to be open and vulnerable but also remaining mindful of patterns or inconsistencies that could indicate unreliability. This practice honors both your desire for connection and your need for self-respect and security.

Trust as an Expression of Self and Integrity

Viewing trust as an art means that each act of trust is not simply a decision but an **expression of who you are and what you stand for**. Trust, when practiced thoughtfully, reflects your commitment to wisdom, resilience, and ethical strength in every connection. This approach to trust turns it into a reflection of your values and personal standards, making it a way to live authentically in an ethically complex world.

Why It Matters: When trust is grounded in self-awareness and integrity, it becomes a powerful tool for building a life aligned with your values. Trust becomes not only a way to connect with others but also a way to honor yourself and your standards.

Example: If honesty and fairness are essential to you, you might choose to extend trust to those who demonstrate these qualities consistently. When trust is built on aligned values, it reinforces your integrity and strengthens the bonds that genuinely matter, allowing you to walk away from connections that don't align with your principles.

Building Connections with Resilience and Adaptability

Trust as an art form requires **resilience and adaptability**. In an unethical world, circumstances may change, and even those you trust may falter. An artful approach to trust means that you are flexible enough to adapt to changing dynamics without becoming overly guarded or resentful. This resilience allows you to maintain your commitment to trust while adjusting expectations when needed.

Why It Matters: Adaptability in trust allows you to engage fully in relationships while remaining prepared for inevitable complexities. It helps you navigate betrayals or disappointments with grace, knowing that trust is not static and can be revisited as necessary.

Example: In a leadership role, you may trust your team members but remain open to adjusting expectations based on performance or communication. This resilience ensures that trust is flexible, capable of responding to real circumstances rather than rigid expectations.

A Balanced Approach: Honoring Trust and Integrity

In a world where ethical clarity is often uncertain, the art of trust lies in **finding a balance that honors both your desire to connect and your need for integrity**. By trusting with a sense of purpose and awareness, you engage in relationships without compromising your values or boundaries. Trust becomes not a leap of blind faith but a balanced approach, a mindful expression of who you are and what you value.

Engaging with Openness and Discernment: When trust is an art, you can approach relationships with openness while using discernment to protect yourself. This balance allows you to enjoy the richness of connection while ensuring that your trust aligns with what you stand for.

Creating Meaningful, Lasting Bonds: Relationships grounded in an artful approach to trust are more likely to withstand challenges. They are built on a foundation of gradual trust, shared values, and mutual respect, which provides resilience and depth.

Living with Integrity in a Complex World: Trust, when approached thoughtfully, reflects a commitment to live with integrity even when circumstances are uncertain. This commitment influences others, fostering a culture of intentional trust that upholds ethical strength and honesty.

Trust as an Artful Practice in Daily Life

This artful approach to trust can be practiced daily, helping you navigate interactions and decisions with intentionality and clarity. Each time you engage in trust thoughtfully, you are choosing to approach life in a way that is **grounded, resilient, and true to yourself**. In every interaction, trust becomes a reflection of the values that matter most to you, guiding you through both simple and complex relationships with grace and self-assurance.

In an uncertain world, trust as an art form is a **way of living that merges courage with caution, openness with boundaries, and authenticity with discernment**. This balanced approach to trust empowers you to build connections that are both resilient and meaningful, creating a life that is not only full of integrity but also deeply fulfilling. Through this personal philosophy, you cultivate a trust that not only withstands the complexities of today's world but also enhances your sense of self and your impact on those around you.

Acknowledgments

This book, *Never Trust Without Doubt: The Interplay Between Doubt and Trust in an Unethical World*, represents an exploration of how trust and doubt coexist as essential partners in navigating complex relationships and decisions. The ideas presented here are rooted in original thought and a deep understanding of human behavior, shaped by observing the challenges we face in extending trust in today's ethically ambiguous world.

I owe immense gratitude to the countless thinkers, leaders, and individuals—whether directly or indirectly—who have inspired this work through their insights on trust, skepticism, and human connection. Their contributions to the broader understanding of these concepts provided the intellectual backdrop against which this book was conceived.

To my readers, I acknowledge the courage it takes to embrace doubt as a companion to trust. This book is dedicated to those who seek to build meaningful relationships and make thoughtful decisions without compromising their values or integrity.

Lastly, I wish to honor the role of doubt itself, a force that challenges us to look beyond surface assumptions, question the obvious, and seek clarity before offering trust. In this way, doubt is not a barrier but a guide, one that makes trust stronger and more enduring.

With deep appreciation,

Sandeep Chavan

About the Author

Sandeep Chavan is an experienced educator, counselor, and industrial engineer with over two decades of professional experience. Combining his engineering background with a passion for understanding human behavior, Sandeep has dedicated much of his career to exploring the dynamics of trust, decision-making, and ethical challenges in complex environments.

As a thinker and writer, Sandeep brings a unique perspective to contemporary issues, blending analytical rigor with deep philosophical insight. His work is rooted in original thought and real-world observations, offering readers practical tools and transformative ideas to navigate trust in an increasingly unpredictable world.

In *Never Trust Without Doubt: The Interplay Between Doubt and Trust in an Unethical World*, Sandeep delves into the delicate balance between trust and doubt, challenging traditional notions and presenting a fresh philosophy for managing relationships and decisions. Through his writing, he aims to empower individuals to cultivate meaningful connections and make thoughtful, resilient choices in ethically complex settings.

Sandeep's contributions extend beyond writing; as an educator, he has mentored countless students, fostering critical thinking and self-awareness. His multidisciplinary approach reflects his belief in lifelong learning, curiosity, and the pursuit of integrity in both personal and professional life.

This book is an invitation to rethink the way we approach trust, to embrace doubt as a guiding force, and to find strength in balance—a philosophy that Sandeep continues to live and inspire through his work.

Did you love *Never Trust Without Doubt*? Then you should read *Reveal to Shield - Learn the Game of Facades*[1] by SANDEEP CHAVAN!

[2]

Reveal to Shield: Learn the Game of Facades by **Sandeep Chavan** takes readers on an enlightening journey through the intricate landscape of human facades—the social masks we wear to protect ourselves, build relationships, and achieve success in a world driven by expectations and appearances. Blending personal insight with practical wisdom, this book explores the art of managing facades thoughtfully, revealing how they can either enhance our lives or cause us to lose touch with our authentic selves.

The book begins with relatable stories of everyday situations, from workplaces and social gatherings to intimate relationships, where we instinctively wear masks to shield our vulnerabilities or fit in. Chavan examines why we adopt these facades and the toll they can take when used unconsciously. For instance, readers may see themselves in the ambitious young professional

1. https://books2read.com/u/3nkD8P
2. https://books2read.com/u/3nkD8P

wearing a mask of invincibility to climb the corporate ladder, only to find that it distances them from their loved ones and their true aspirations.

Chavan's narrative then shifts to his own transformative journey, beginning as a promising student and dedicated professional, only to grapple with challenges of identity, ambition, and addiction. Through deeply personal anecdotes, he recounts the pressures to conform to societal ideals of success and strength, detailing his journey toward self-awareness. This journey led him to embrace his real passions and ultimately find balance and fulfillment as an educator. He invites readers to reflect on their own lives, asking: *Are my facades helping me grow, or are they holding me back?*

In the latter part of the book, Chavan empowers readers to use facades as tools rather than barriers. With practical advice, he explains how to intentionally adopt facades in ways that are authentic and aligned with one's core values. From the mentor who wears a calm, wise facade to support young learners, to the professional using a confident exterior to lead a team through challenges, **Reveal to Shield** offers insight into balancing personal truth with the demands of modern life.

Designed for anyone seeking a more authentic, balanced life, this book is a thoughtful exploration of how to navigate the roles and expectations placed upon us while staying true to ourselves. With an engaging blend of relatable scenarios, personal reflections, and practical tips, **Reveal to Shield** is a guide for those who wish to live intentionally, connecting deeply with themselves and others. Whether you're striving to find success, meaning, or simply a bit of peace in a busy world, this book is a powerful resource for embracing authenticity while skillfully managing the social dynamics around you.

Read more at www.gyrusvision.com.

Also by SANDEEP CHAVAN

It's Not AI, It's AHI - Amplified Human Intelligence
The Decision Paradox
The Four Sapiens
Malicious Script of Indian Polity
The IIT Legacy & Global Impact
The IIT Legacy & Global Impact
You are just a Version of Your Original
Win the Game You Didn't Choose
Always Keep Your Bags Packed
Reveal to Shield - Learn the Game of Facades
Engage Beyond Elections
Culture, Identity & Change: The Evolution of Indian Society
The Triangular Dynamics
Never Trust Without Doubt

Watch for more at www.gyrusvision.com.

Milton Keynes UK
Ingram Content Group UK Ltd.
UKHW030141051224
452010UK00001B/236